Praise for *The Everyday Fermentation Handbook*

"*The Everyday Fermentation Handbook* is a refreshingly clear guide to the sometimes elusive world of fermentation. From simply elegant (leek rings) to brilliantly bizarre (peanut butter and sauerkraut cream cookies), Branden Byers gives us an honest and creative take on making and using fermented foods at home."

—Benjamin Wolfe, microbiologist at Harvard University and regular contributor to *Lucky Peach*

"With this book, Branden Byers has offered a gateway into the world of fermentation that will calm the fears of new fermenters and help more experienced bacteria-lovers perfect their game. Very specific instructions, lovely photos, and a fascinating breadth of coverage on ferments of all kinds make *The Everyday Fermentation Handbook* a book you can actually use every day. Branden dives in to bubbly vats of well-loved and lesser-known ferments, embodying the spirit of fermentation and experimentation with inventive recipes and a lively exploration of the science behind these exciting foods."

—Amanda Feifer, founder of Phickle.com

"I really enjoy *The Everyday Fermentation Handbook* from fermentation raconteur/ podcaster Branden Byers. This is a great book for anyone who appreciates this eons-old tradition of food preservation, which has been briefly interrupted by the postwar allure of faster-better-cheaper industrial food production and modern conveniences. It provides the reader with the confidence needed to resurrect and make practical (and delicious!) use of these precious cultural traditions."

—Austin Durant, founder of Fermenters Club

"Fermentation is a wonderful and transformative process of food that is easy to embrace for its health-giving properties and exotic taste, but often it can be hard to change our habits to incorporate these in our everyday diet. This is a practical book that gives you inspiration and confidence to do so. It is easy to use for the beginner as well as the more experienced fermenter with good and easy-to-follow recipes."

—Eva Bakkeslett, artist, cultivator, and fermenter

"Branden's knowledge and excitement about the science and flavors of fermented foods is considerable. I've been lucky to witness this enthusiasm spread to others with his teachings of both beginner and advanced-level fermentation topics."

—Philip Crawford, board member of Slow Food Madison and founder of Madison Food Camp

"Branden's new book gives beginners an engaging look at the world of fermented foods, guiding us through simple processes that are easily incorporated into our everyday routines. Step by step, the book inspires us with the confidence to experiment and explore new flavors, textures, and foods we may not be familiar with. Before you know it, your larder will be filled with delicious, healthy kimchi, heirloom yogurts, sourdough breads, and fermented drinks! With more than thirty inventive recipes that make the most of the bright, tart, spicy flavors found in fermented foods, snacks and mealtimes become a whole new adventure. Kimchi Pizza, anyone?"

—Kim Bartko, program director of Good Food Festival

"Byers demystifies the dark art of fermentation, outlining techniques and processes using plain English in an affable, approachable voice. Newcomers to the world of controlled rot will be inspired into action starting with simple and accessible projects like sauerkraut and yogurt, but by casting a global net, Byers offers up a world of inspiration for even experienced fermenters."

—Sean Timberlake, founder of Punk Domestics

DEDICATION

For my son, Adrian. When he is old enough to read this dedication, may he think it special; when he's old enough to comprehend this, may he know how much I love him; and if he goes on to be a father himself one day, may he finally realize how indebted I am to him for being a relatively patient baby as I fermented, cooked, and wrote this book.

Published by
Adams Media, a division of F+W Media, Inc.
57 Littlefield Street, Avon, MA 02322. U.S.A.
www.adamsmedia.com

ISBN 10: 1-4405-7366-2
ISBN 13: 978-1-4405-7366-8
eISBN 10: 1-4405-7367-0
eISBN 13: 978-1-4405-7367-5

Printed in the United States of America.

10 9 8 7 6 5 4 3 2 1

Readers are urged to take all appropriate precautions before undertaking any how-to task. Always read and follow instructions and safety warnings for all tools and materials, and call in a professional if the task stretches your abilities too far. Although every effort has been made to provide the best possible information in this book, neither the publisher nor the author are responsible for accidents, injuries, or damage incurred as a result of tasks undertaken by readers. This book is not a substitute for professional services.

Always follow safety and commonsense cooking protocol while using kitchen utensils, operating ovens and stoves, and handling uncooked food. If children are assisting in the preparation of any recipe, they should always be supervised by an adult.

Many of the designations used by manufacturers and sellers to distinguish their product are claimed as trademarks. Where those designations appear in this book and F+W Media, Inc. was aware of a trademark claim, the designations have been printed with initial capital letters.

Photos by Branden Byers.
Cover and book design by Sylvia McArdle.
Cover image by Branden Byers.

This book is available at quantity discounts for bulk purchases.
For information, please call 1-800-289-0963.

From the creator of
FermUp.com

The Everyday
FERMENTATION
Handbook

A REAL-LIFE GUIDE TO FERMENTING FOOD–
without Losing Your Mind or Your Microbes

BRANDEN BYERS

Adamsmedia
Avon, Massachusetts

CONTENTS

Introduction

Fermentation is everywhere. It's a natural process, and humans, over the ages, have managed to control enough of the process in order to make a few delicious and healthy foods.

It's a great way to get healthy foods into your diet. Of course, you can buy some fermented foods in the store, and probably do; your shopping list undoubtedly includes things like pickles and possibly sauerkraut. However, in this book you'll find recipes free of preservatives and artificial ingredients for these delicious treats—much healthier than anything you can buy in a store. There are other health benefits: For example, as you'll see later, fermentation breaks down lactose in dairy products.

Fermenting can preserve foods. Not surprisingly, many of the recipes for fermenting were first developed at a time when most humans didn't have access to refrigeration. Fermentation was a way around this problem. Today, it can make storing foods much simpler.

Finally, of course, fermented foods are delicious and fun. We live in an age of refrigeration and highly processed foods. Most people are no longer required to preserve food in times of abundance in order to be able to survive extended periods of scarcity such as long winters. Now most humans can ferment food as a luxury.

I love fermented foods because I get to play amateur scientist in my kitchen. Learning about new ferments from around the world is an opportunity for me to explore where these foods originated and the necessity or desires that once shaped the fermentation process. And of course there are the flavors; although a picky eater as a child, I now crave the complex, intense, and sometimes funky flavors of fermented foods.

With all of this comes the opportunity to share knowledge with others. What were once commonplace traditions, passed down from one generation to the next, have in many cases been lost. The invention of alternatives and conveniences over the past couple hundred years has meant too few parents and grandparents handing down the skills of fermentation to the next generation.

While fermented foods can be purchased from commercial producers, it's possible to make a lot more than what can be found in the grocery store. Some fermented foods are too strange for mass appeal and so are relegated to limited regions or not produced commercially at all.

Fermented foods don't require specialized equipment, they offer endless possibilities, and often they're less expensive to make than buy.

For most people, the hardest part is figuring out where to store ferments in progress and how to plan ahead so that fermented foods are ready to eat when desired. It's disappointing to crave sauerkraut or kimchi and then realize that either the next batch still has two weeks to finish or that you never started it in the first place. Even worse is to lose a starter culture of sourdough or heirloom yogurt that can't be easily replaced. Throughout this book you will find tips and suggestions to ensure you have fermented food ready to serve whenever you so desire.

Whether you are looking for ways to incorporate one or one hundred different homemade fermented foods into your life, the recipes in this book will help you get started. Fermentation does take time and patience but the learning curve is gradual. Start simple with something that sounds appetizing and the next thing you know, you may have a zoo of microbial diversity fermenting in your home, too. Enter the world of fermentation and you will never feel alone in the kitchen again.

PART 1

THE BASICS

These first chapters will give you a basic understanding of fermentation and an overview of the general techniques used throughout this book. If you decide to jump directly to the recipes, then refer to this section if specific directions confuse you.

Part I will show you how to ferment specific foods and provide you with a selection of recipes to inspire your own future fermented concoctions.

Chapter 1

FERMENTATION 101

Fermentation is a process of microbial transformation. Microbes pre-digest food, create new flavors, and protect against food spoilage. This transformation is sometimes subtle and mellow whereas at other times it is loud and in your face.

To Cook or Not to Cook

The term "cook" is used loosely in this context. Not all of the recipes that you'll find later in this book require the application of heat, but many do. Heat will kill many of the living microbes in fermented foods. If you wish to eat all of your ferments raw, then consider some of the heated creations, because a few of these recipes allow for the addition of fermented ingredients at the end of the cooking process and therefore will still preserve microbial life.

I eat both raw and cooked varieties of fermented foods. Bread is a great example of a fermented food: The first stage uses the transformative actions of fermentation, but the final product is a baked ghost town of once-active microbes. I don't imagine there are many people touting the health benefits of unbaked bread.

What about ferments such as sauerkraut or kimchi? I love to eat fermented vegetables raw, but I'm not afraid to cook with them either. They can add such complex flavors to food that I would be neglecting an entire genre of ingredients if I abstained from heat.

In addition, science is still discovering more about the probiotic effects of fermented foods. While living microorganisms may or may not have specific health benefits, the same may also one day be found to be true of recently deceased microbes. If microbial life forms can communicate with each other, is it possible that they could also extract information from the remains of dead microbes passing through the digestive tract in order to better ward off attacks from competing microbes?

This seems plausible considering the wealth of knowledge gleaned by humans when uncovering archaeological remains of past civilizations. Granted, I also have a tendency of anthropomorphizing microbes in order to better explain them, and at times, this probably has the opposite effect of distancing myself from the truth.

I imagine the microbiome of my gut as a communication hub of microbes traversing between the equivalence of entire galaxies. These space travelers freely share information amongst each other as they pass through the digestive track. Some may stick around longer, sharing extensive accounts of current events from the outside world, whereas others may heed warnings of potential threats in the last moments of their lives before being consumed by a hostile environment.

Other dead microbes may pass through, sharing only the remains of their short lives. And yet, these microbial remains could offer a glimpse or hint, at times, more valuable than any of their living brethren could convey. The more information exchanged, in theory, the more appropriate the defense against microbes will be.

Even without much evidence (yet) to back up my imagination, I still eat my fermented foods cooked as well as raw. This approach covers my health bases while providing me the opportunity to not only enjoy the transformational flavors of fermentation but also the dramatic flavors of cooking with these same ferments.

However you ultimately enjoy your ferments and the act of fermentation, you are about to start consciously collaborating with microbes. No longer need you fear these bugs. Set aside memories of fear-mongering commercials and advertisements demonizing bacteria. There may be a few bad seeds, but most of the microbes around you are your friends. Feed them, and they will provide you with delicacy.

Touched by Fermentation

Fermentation is a microbial process of transformation. Once thought of as magic, or gifts from gods, fermentation changes food in predictable, yet surprising, ways. The ordinary vegetable is transformed into a delectable sour and nutritious treat; milk is converted from a highly perishable food source into something capable of, in some cases, being stored for years; and grains, fruits, and honey have affected human consciousness for ages by turning sugars into ethanol. All this happens through the powers of microbial transformation.

Microbes and food go together like a horse and carriage (unless you find carriages demeaning for horses, in which case they go together like peanut butter and jelly).

Technically, fermentation refers to, in part, the breakdown of organic matter in an anaerobic (oxygen-free) environment by means of yeast or bacteria. In colloquial terms, the fermentation of food incorporates not only bacteria and yeast but also molds. It occurs in both anaerobic and aerobic processes. If microbes mingle with food long enough, that food will end up fermented, contaminated, or rotten.

Fermented foods straddle the line between fresh and rotten. Where people draw that line depends on many factors including cultural upbringing, experience, and taste. What is a divine delicacy to one may be repulsive to another. Most fermented foods and beverages fall between such extremes; the majority of humans consume multiple forms of fermentation daily, whether they know it or not.

If you happen to enjoy bread, yogurt, beer, wine, coffee, chocolate, or vinegar, then you have been touched by fermentation. It is nearly inescapable, but in modern society most people are oblivious to the microbial diversity all around them. Even worse, much of the world fears that which cannot be seen. But the reality is that the majority of the bacteria and fungi in and around us cause humans no harm. Confusion escalates with the fact that some so-called "bad" bacteria are harmful in some instances, benign in others, and at times, even helpful.

Despising and fearing microbes is, in essence, a naive loathing of oneself. While still in its infancy, human microbiome research explores the communities of microbes in and on our bodies. We are teeming with microbes, and so are most other forms of life on this planet (exceptions being such animals as the germ-free laboratory mouse). Microbial cells outnumber human cells ten to one. From a certain perspective, we are more microbe than human. You—quite literally—are what you eat.

Throughout history, humans have eaten a lot of microbes, but over the past few decades, processed foods have been wiping out populations of microbes we once regularly consumed. Pasteurization and sterilization have undoubtedly saved many lives, but because of the effort to keep food shelf stable, much of what's sold is lifeless and microbe free.

This provides a new lens through which to examine modern-day health issues. In fact, there is already growing evidence that living food is generally healthy food, and continual consumption of dead and sterile food isn't nearly as nutritious.

However, health and diet aren't the only reasons to seek out fermentation. Fermented foods taste delicious too. These aren't foods you have to choke down for a diet; they're something to be cherished, explored, and celebrated. Whatever your reason for fermentation, get ready for a wild microbial transformation in your kitchen, on your tongue, and deep down in your gut.

Decay: It's What's for Dinner

Decay and dinner? It's unusual to use these words together in a sentence. And for good reason; eating decayed and rotten foods can be dangerous, right up there with deadly berries and mushrooms. The term "food-poisoning" brings to mind a vision of contaminated (not even necessarily rotten) food as a bottle labeled with a skull and crossbones. Most people don't die from food poisoning but the threat is real. While the industrialization of food has done much to shelter the modern human from the reality of food, it still remains that eating food is a risky endeavor. Even with today's scientific understanding of contamination, food-borne illness remains a threat around the globe.

Fermentation is a form of decomposition, a type of controlled rot. By controlling the environment in which microbes and food interact, it is possible to regulate how food rots in predictable ways. These predictable forms of transformation result in food that is not only safe to eat but also desirable.

With proper understanding and knowledge of a few basic principles, humans have harnessed the power of beneficial microbes to protect them from harmful, deadly, and putrefying microorganisms. Humans have been able to do this through observation and experimentation well before anyone even comprehended the existence of microscopic life forms.

If you have a blanket fear of all microorganisms, then it might be time to reevaluate a few assumptions. Beyond food, if it weren't for microbial decomposition, we would live in a drastically different world (if it were even possible to inhabit such a world). There are specialist microbes of all orders, and these bacteria and fungi are the great recyclers of our planet.

Throughout the earth's evolution, as new organic materials formed, different microbes evolved to metabolize and break down these materials. This is a common feature of the natural world. When there is an abundance of a resource, especially a food source, something will eventually come along to reap its benefits, unlock some of the stored energy, and continue the circle of life.

While it may be hard to imagine, there was a time before any microbe could decompose wood. This is because plants did not evolve to form woody compounds until conifer shrubs and trees began to transform the landscape many hundreds of millions of years ago. Once this new material appeared, something evolved to eat it: a wood-rotting fungus. If it, or some other species hadn't evolved a way to digest the components of wood, fallen trees would have littered the landscape offering little opportunity for new soil development or future generations of trees, plants, and animals. This cycle of decomposition provides a means for new life and growth built upon dead organic matter.

The food that humans consume is full of organic matter ripe for decomposition. If we don't eat it, a microbe surely will, as can be attested by anyone that has witnessed the transformation of a compost pile into soil or forgotten food in the back of a refrigerator. But fresh is not the only way to enjoy food. If we wait to consume certain foods, while at the same time providing proper environments for specific bacteria and fungi, we can enjoy fermented products that are far more flavorful than their fresh counterparts.

This process can also keep a food from decaying further. Throughout history, fermentation has been used as a form of preservation. Because we provide desirable microbes a home in our foods, these same microbes help to create a hostile environment for undesirable organisms, thereby slowing down the process of further decomposition.

In some fermented foods, such as bread or yogurt, the amount of decomposition is minimal. However, certain other dairy, vegetable, grain, legume, and meat ferments have ventured much further from fresh. Part acquired taste, part cultural framework, and part weird fetishizing: The fact is that humans generally like stinky foods. It just depends on which ones you're willing, or able, to consume.

The more you ferment, the more you may surprise yourself as to what you begin to crave. Something that once seemed weird may soon become awesome. The kimchi fermenting in your cupboard may smell odd the first time, but by the third or fourth batch it may well smell like a microbial perfume, one that you eagerly anticipate inhaling every time you walk by. Other ferments may smell bad while they're developing, but the taste is well worth the assault on your nasal passageways.

The vast majority of ferments in this book will fall into the category of non-gross and surprisingly tasty. One of the pleasures of fermenting your own foods is the opportunity to discover what level of fermentation for each food that you like best. You may enjoy yogurt after fermenting for only a few hours (something I can't deal with due to my lactose intolerance) or may prefer sauerkraut that has fermented slowly in a basement for months.

We each have our own tolerances and preferences for taste, texture, and decay. The recipes and instructions throughout this book offer a starting point but are by no means the final word. Once you grasp the basic concepts of fermentation, you will be free to choose your own fermentation adventures.

Fast Food Fermentation

Yes, the idea of fast fermentation is a bit of an oxymoron. Fermentation takes time. It is a slow microbial process. But most of the work is done by the microbes and not by you. Most fermentation prep is brief, whereas the wait is long.

With some ferments, the chopping and dicing of vegetables becomes repetitive. This is a good reason to invite a group of friends or family to make larger batches of ferments together. Lively conversation passes the time much more quickly. As fermenting foods build communities of microbes, so, too, do they provide an opportunity to unite communities of people. Fermentation is about culture and culture is about community. Fermentation warrants sharing.

Fermentation is not a fast food kind of fare. Instead, it takes time, requires patience, and occasionally, after long periods of waiting, ends up not tasting quite as expected. Fermentation is about the journey. While the destination offers flavors found nowhere else in the culinary world, it is the transformations of food, microbe, and eater along the way that offer true satisfaction.

What mesmerizing power such transformation must have exerted before the age of science and knowledge of microbes. The work of fermentation was once an act of magic or gods. How else to explain a simple food left to sit for a period of time that developed into a taste of magnificent splendor?

Some foods are begging to be fermented, and once you try them, there will be little chance of turning back. Whether you want to unlock otherwise inaccessible nutrients, flood the microbiome with fresh microorganisms, or change the mundane into the monumental, fermentation is a form of kitchen alchemy available to anyone. It may not be the fastest process in the culinary world, but it sure is rewarding.

Are you ready?

Easy Fermentation

Even if fermentation isn't generally considered fast, one thing that most ferments have in common is their ease of preparation. Microbes do most of the work; all you have to do is provide them the proper environment for success. It's one of those "if you build it, they will ferment it" kind of things.

The fermented foods in this book are simple to prepare at home. Vegetables are by far the easiest and make a good starting point if you've never fermented before. They are easy because the lactic acid bacteria that we want to cultivate are already present on the surface of vegetables.

These bacteria are salt tolerant, whereas many microbes can't stand the stuff. We provide the lactic acid bacteria a comfy salt brine in order to weed out competition and allow our bacteria to expand and proliferate. The lactic acid bacteria do their thing, creating a sour flavor that further protects the vegetables from competing microbes. It's a win/win situation; the lactic acid bacteria get to multiply, and we get tasty vegetables that last longer than their fresh counterparts.

Dairy ferments are also easy but most of the time, instead of relying on native bacteria in the milk, we inoculate pasteurized milk with additional microbes. Raw milk from healthy cows, like raw vegetables, has native populations of bacteria that are ready to ferment if given the chance. Yet these populations aren't always the microbes needed for certain types of dairy fermentation. Much of this stems from the fact that we are trying to culture styles of milk from other cultures or geographical regions. The cows, goats, and sheep of differing locales may have differing native populations of microbes.

If you want to create a yogurt or cheese from a specific region, you may need a starter culture. Once you obtain a starter culture, dairy fermentation, such as yogurt and cultured butter, is easy. Cheese making can be easy or challenging. This book will cover a few of the easier ones.

Legume fermentation is simple and easy to understand and perform but requires a few more tools to get the job done. That is, unless you live in an environment similar in climate to the original geographic region of any given ferment.

Tempeh is easy if you live in Indonesia or Hawaii because the temperature and humidity are already at ideal levels. When I make tempeh in the middle of a Wisconsin winter, I must incubate the ferment at higher temperatures and humidity in order to achieve an edible end product. More on incubators, tools, and techniques to follow.

The most challenging aspect of legume fermentation is that it often includes molds in the fermentation process. These are not molds that are signs of spoilage; these are friendly. Molds may be fuzzy, but they can also be fussy. They generally take a little more babysitting, but who doesn't love a cute little fuzzy baby monster mold? The ever-so-slightly more required attention is worth it. Like so many other fuzzy pets, once you bring one home, even if it's more work than expected, it works its way into your heart. Once you have some experience with other ferments, open up and let some legume mold into your home.

As for beverage fermentation, it is nearly as easy as vegetable fermentation. At least, it starts that way. Molds aren't the only thing that can be fussy; so can people as they concoct elaborate strategies for creating absolute perfection in alcoholic beverages.

In this book we will focus on the simpler alcoholic and nonalcoholic beverages. Some require a starter culture and others "catch" native bacteria and yeast in the environment to do the busy work of converting sugars. They may not all be as fancy, but they still taste complex and refreshing. If you really get into beverage fermentation, there are countless resources available for further research.

Even easier than fermentation itself is incorporating fermented foods into your cooking and eating habits. Some of the recipes in this book are easier to accomplish with special tools—a pasta machine is quicker and more efficient than a rolling pin—but these gadgets aren't necessary if you're willing to take a bit more time and work a little harder.

In some of the recipes, such as the process of making cultured butter, I even recommend a more labor-intensive process so you can fully experience the physical transformations of "churning" cultured cream into a solid product. Sometimes I find it easier to start with a more elementary approach, gain knowledge, and then make the decision to either keep doing it using more time and labor or skip ahead using specialized tools.

No matter your previous experience, you're sure to find plenty of recipes to fit your comfort level. Everyone's definition of easy is different, but I think you will soon find that fermentation and cooking with ferments can be as easy as (hard cider) pie.

Structured Fermentation

Without structure, it is easy to get behind on your schedule of making and enjoying fermented foods. Lives get busy and ferments get forgotten. You don't attribute convenience, instant gratification, and speed to fermented foods. In that respect, much of modern society goes against the grain of fermentation. For this reason, building and maintaining a habit of fermentation takes conscious effort.

Of course, that's the case when forming any habit whether it grows from interest or necessity. When I first began fermenting foods, it was difficult for me to build regularity around my then-newfound hobby. My fermentation schedule was erratic and without regard to which ferments I would have ready to eat at any given time. I started plenty of ferments but I also lost sourdough and yogurt starter cultures because I did not properly maintain feeding schedules.

Think of fermentation as cultivating a microbial garden. The planning, planting, and tending of garden plants parallels the planning, inoculating, and monitoring involved in fermentation.

As has already been discussed, fermentation is inherently easy, and humans only make it difficult if they choose to do so. When you begin your fermentation adventure, start simple, making a few ferments that you're excited about.

After you've successfully fermented a few batches, consider how much of any given ferment you would like to eat on a regular basis. Then plan a realistic fermentation schedule that fits your needs. Maybe using only in-season produce from the store, market, or your garden is important to you. If so, you will need to harvest or purchase your green beans in season and preserve them through the winter.

It is not necessary to ferment in large batches to have a steady supply of fermented foods. If saving space is more important to you than seasonality, scheduling a weekly ten-minute vegetable chop-and-pack session can keep your refrigerator or pantry stocked but not overflowing. Or, instead, focus on dairy and beverage fermentations that necessitate regular upkeep of small batches.

The important point to remember when planning fermentation is that just like a garden, things take time to grow and foods take time to ferment. Know when you want to eat your ferments and understand how long they will take to make.

It's just like preparing a turkey for a Thanksgiving feast. Don't plan and your guests may be eating side dishes all day until that big bird finally cooks through. The only difference with fermented foods is that instead of planning hours in advance, we're talking days, weeks, or months. This might seem daunting at first, but so is the first time cooking a turkey. After a few Thanksgivings, there's nothing to it.

Of course, if structure really isn't your way, feel free to slap a few ferments together whenever your ferment muse comes a-calling.

The Comic Cowboy Space Travelers of the Microbial Universe

Who or what are these mysterious microbes that lurk amongst fermented foods? How can you differentiate between friend and foe? I like to think of microbes as the superheroes and villains of a microscopic universe. They may not be as black and white as the good-versus-evil world of comic books, but they certainly seem to have superpowers.

And for good reason. Imagine a world where new land or uncharted territory is discovered regularly. Fresh food is ripe territory for microbial invasions. It's like a perpetual Wild West with rival cowboys and profiteers competing with each other for riches and resources or intergalactic space travel with an abundance of empty, yet habitable, planets that are free for the taking. Except, of course, there are countless alien species likely to discover such planets at the same moment. The frenzy to compete begins.

As exciting and chaotic as this may sound, the interplay of these comic cowboy space travelers is generally a repetitive sequence of actions. Of course, after you've seen a few microbial blockbusters the stories become predictable. On the microbial scale (and within the short microbial lifespan) these organisms are using all of their powers, ammunition, and prowess in order to outcompete each other, but the pattern of events is still foreseeable.

When it comes to fermented foods, this predictability is a good thing. It means that if you follow the general guidelines throughout this book, then you will most likely succeed in your fermentation projects with few, if any, contaminants or failed ferments. This is especially true when dealing with vegetable ferments; it is very difficult to completely screw up. Sure, sometimes the flavor or texture isn't exactly to your liking, but with a bit of troubleshooting and a few tweaks, problems are easily corrected in subsequent batches.

My analogy of war and competition offers an anthropomorphic view of microbes, and a rather barbaric one at that. For all I know, these microbes may resolve their territorial disputes through diplomacy, treaties, and hugs. The only snag in this analogy is that a lot of microbes die in the process of fermentation so unless I find out that these microbes are actually martyrs, I'll stick with my comic book notions.

The Main Players

Now let's look at some of the most important figures in this drama.

BACTERIA

There are countless bacteria involved in the many different styles of fermentation. But the main group of players that you should know as a beginner is lumped together under the classification of lactic acid bacteria, often referred to as LAB. Each subset of the LAB has differing traits, but overall, they are salt-tolerant, acid-producing little buggers. They are some of the nicest and most beneficial bacteria found in fermented foods.

A few bacteria, such as *Bacillus subtilis*, are good in some foods and not in others. If you start making koji, then you do not want *Bacillus subtilis* in your rice (generally its presence results from too high an incubation temperature) or they will dominate and outcompete the koji molds. On the other hand, nattō is made from soybeans fermented with *Bacillus subtilis* creating a sticky, slimy texture and mild ammonia aroma.

YEAST

The title of Most Famous Yeast goes to *Saccharomyces cerevisiae*. It has been studied and cultivated more than any other yeast. It's used in winemaking, bread baking, beer brewing, and beyond.

However, don't let this famous yeast overshadow all its hardworking compatriots. Wild yeast, differing by region or environment, can be found in sourdough bread and alcoholic beverages that have been spontaneously fermented. Kefir grains are an example of a symbiotic colony of bacteria and yeast (referred to as a SCOBY) that work in harmony to ferment milk.

Whichever the yeast, its main importance is in converting sugars to ethanol and one of its byproducts is carbon dioxide. This process converts sugary liquids, such as grape juice or malted grains, into alcoholic beverages. The production of carbon dioxide leads to the ability to naturally carbonate fermented beverages in sealed vessels.

MOLDS

Mold fermentation was less common in the western world until recently. Foods such as sake, miso, amazake, and soy sauce are made possible through the enzymes created by the mold *Aspergillus oryzae*. This mold is used to ferment grains, such as rice and barley, or legumes such as soybeans, in order to create enzymes with the ability to break down carbohydrates and proteins, thus creating ideal environments for other microbes to continue the fermentation process.

A world-famous mold of Indonesia, *Rhizopus oligosporus*, is used for fermenting soybeans into tempeh. The mycelium (sort of like fungal roots) of *Rhizopus oligosporus* bond the soybeans, or other legumes, into a firm cake that can then be cut up and consumed or cooked.

Friendly molds are a wonderful way to break down legumes into a more digestible and quicker-to-cook food. In addition, they create beautiful branches of fuzz that quickly cover whatever they are fermenting. It is one of the more visually exciting and rewarding food transformations I've ever witnessed.

Spontaneous Fermentation Versus Starter Cultures

To starter-culture, or not to starter-culture, that is the question. Whether it is nobler to wild ferment or inoculate depends upon the ferment and you. Neither method is inherently right nor wrong, but they each have pros, cons, and neutralities.

"Wild fermentation," a term made popular by Sandor Katz's 2003 book of the same title, allows for native bacteria, yeast, and molds to colonize foods and beverages to be fermented. These native microbes are found in the air, in the environment, on hands, on utensils, and in the fresh foods themselves. By providing the ideal environment (i.e., salt, water, temperature) for fermentation, the desired microbes gain the upper hand (no, microbes do not actually have hands) against competing microbes, thereby protecting the food or beverage from contamination. In essence, leave prepared food to sit and it will ferment naturally.

Starter cultures, on the other hand, leave less to chance. A starter culture is a community of microbes used to inoculate a food or beverage in order to provide a strong colony that will outcompete undesirable microbes. These colonies sometimes only consist of one or a few different strains of bacteria, yeast, or molds that have been isolated in laboratories with specific and consistent traits.

Isolated starter cultures, often referred to as direct-set cultures, are very useful in a commercial environment where consistency and exacting predictability equals higher profits. Some ferments throughout this book, such as cheese or nattō, generally require one of these types of starter cultures in order to produce the desired ferment.

Yet, not all starter cultures are isolated in laboratories. Some, such as kombucha or kefir, are used in the form of a symbiotic colony of bacteria and yeast (SCOBY). Such SCOBYs originally formed through a process of spontaneous fermentation. Once humans realized the potential of these SCOBYs, they were saved and reused to make future batches of our favorite fermented foods and beverages.

Another form of starter culture that is not derived from a laboratory is introduced by the act of backslopping. In this process a small portion of the previous ferment is used to inoculate future generations of the same ferment. Backslopping is the technique used for all heirloom yogurts in this book and before microbiologists came along it was the main option if you were using a starter culture.

Backslopping is also used when the fermenter introduces a portion of his or her previous vegetable brine into the next batch of fermented vegetables. While it's not backslopping, a very similar technique uses a brine, whey, or dairy ferment from a different type of ferment in order to jump-start the fermentation process. Some people use whey (a byproduct of dairy fermentation) to inoculate a vegetable ferment in this fashion. I don't believe there is a proper term for this quasi-backslop method. Let's call it fast-forward-slopping since it is used to speed up spontaneous fermentation.

The important takeaway, in regard to how wild or domesticated cultures affect you as an up-and-coming fermentation master, is this: If a fermentation process calls for spontaneous fermentation, then don't add a starter; but if a starter is required, then you will need to obtain the culture by mail (either purchased from a website or through an online culture exchange), or if you are lucky, from one of your local fermentation buddies.

Remember, many starter cultures continue to grow and expand. If you are the first person in your circle of friends and family to obtain a starter culture for heirloom yogurt, kombucha, dairy kefir, water kefir, ginger beer plant, or any other non-direct-set culture, be sure to spread the love. Think of it as your duty, following in the footsteps of previous fermenters who did the same throughout history. Also, you'll be grateful that you did if you ever accidentally neglect one of your cultures and need a new one after it dies. Cultures sometimes die, but their fermentation superpowers can live on if shared.

With great power comes great responsibility, and so, be certain to share your starter cultures with others so that the world may never be without such ferments.

Equipment

You don't need much in order to begin fermenting foods at home. On the extreme end, you can ferment cabbage by digging a hole in the ground and tearing the leaves with your bare hands. Sure, you might end up with a bit of dirt on the outer edges, but with proper application of salt, and possibly some mud or clay sealant on the sides, you'll have an edible product. Fermentation really can be that basic.

However, most humans have progressed beyond pit fermentation to using some form of fermentation vessel. If you have a glass jar or ceramic crock then you already have a vessel. Some are fancier than others, but any clean container will work.

Here's a list of fermentation supplies and kitchen tools to consider.

FERMENTATION VESSELS

Fermenting in glass jars is a common practice. Quart and half-gallon Mason jars are readily available and relatively inexpensive. Ceramic crocks and gallon-size jars work great for larger batches. More advanced options include airlock systems in order to create fully anaerobic environments. While offering convenience, these are not necessary when starting out and many people never ferment vegetables under airlocks. Anything that can hold water can be used as a fermentation vessel. Feel free to use your imagination.

KNIVES

A good and sharp chef's knife or Santoku knife will do wonders in the kitchen. Chopping is a large part of vegetable fermentation and dull knives can quickly turn a fermentation adventure into a seemingly endless chore.

CUTTING BOARDS

I recommend using a separate cutting board for preparing vegetables. I use both plastic and wood cutting boards. Wood cutting boards need replacing less often but good ones cost more upfront compared to inexpensive plastic boards.

GRATERS

For most fermented vegetables, I prefer to use a knife. But grating some items such as carrots can provide a different texture than julienned or thinly sliced. You may also wish to grate your own cheeses.

FOOD PROCESSOR

I don't generally use a food processor when preparing vegetables for fermentation, but I do use one frequently when cooking or baking with fermented foods. Some of the recipes in this book call for a food processor, but most also provide alternative suggestions such as knives or pestles and mortars.

STRAINERS

Mesh strainers are especially helpful when making kefir. According to much lore on the Internet, a nylon mesh strainer is better than a stainless steel one, but I have used both nylon and stainless steel over the years without noticeable harm to cultures. Just remember that prolonged contact between metal and acidic ferments can be corrosive, but in general, brief contact such as straining is inconsequential.

DIGITAL GRAM SCALES

Some forms of fermentation and baking require more accuracy than others. Gram scales provide accuracy beyond measuring spoons or cups since ingredient density can fluctuate depending on where the item was sourced, how it was scooped, or even the humidity level in the environment in which you're measuring. For best accuracy, get two scales: one that can measure down to a tenth of a gram and another that measures large quantities.

DIGITAL THERMOMETERS

For some ferments, such as in cheese, koji, nattō, and tempeh making, it will be very useful to take accurate temperature readings. While analog thermometers will work, they are slower to respond and require more frequent calibration. I use digital thermometers for many projects in my kitchen and fermentation lab but they aren't absolutely necessary. People made cheese and other ferments before thermometers were available. However, they will make the beginner's life easier.

PH METER

Only one recipe in this book—Mozzarella (see Chapter 3)—would greatly benefit from a reliable pH meter. Mozzarella will only stretch when at a proper temperature and pH. The recipe in this book gives directions for making the cheese without a meter, but if you already have one or are considering purchasing one, then your mozzarella life will be easier.

CHEESECLOTH

You'll need regular cheesecloth and butter muslin for making strained yogurts and cheeses. Butter muslin has a tighter weave and will be appropriate for the recipes in this book. Most cheesecloth found at grocery stores will be too coarse a weave for straining yogurt or soft cheese. Fabric muslin or even a pillowcase will work if you can't find butter muslin.

AIRLOCKS

Go to any local beer- or wine-making shop and you are sure to find airlocks. They are useful when an anaerobic environment is required. Some people use airlocks attached to glass jars when fermenting vegetables, but a completely anaerobic environment in those instances isn't necessary (although convenient). Airlocks are most important in the later stages of wild alcohol fermentation. Once a sugary beverage has attracted wild yeast, placing an airlock on a jug keeps unwanted bacteria away from the accumulating alcohol and remaining sugars. If alcohol is left to the open air, acetobacter bacteria will convert the alcohol to vinegar.

PRESSURE COOKER

Pressure cookers aren't just for canning. They work great for quickly preparing soybeans for tempeh or miso. They can also steam rice for making large batches of koji. While not necessary, they can save a lot of energy and time if you plan to make certain ferments regularly.

INCUBATORS

All ferments have temperature requirements in order to produce a good quality fermented food. But a few ferments have a much narrower range of acceptable temperatures. These ferments, such as Bulgarian yogurt, koji, tempeh, and nattō can be difficult to produce without some form of artificial incubation. Sometimes an insulated cooler is enough to keep a ferment at ideal temperature, but other times you need a more specific degree of accuracy. In these instances, incubators can be made at home using temperature controllers, light bulbs, and insulated containers. Other options include dehydrators and heating pads. For instructions on how to build an incubator, go to *www.fermup.com/incubators*.

TEMPERATURE CONTROLLERS

I find temperature controllers indispensable. In conjunction with an insulated box or unused refrigerator and a heat source, I am able to accurately control temperature. This makes for much more consistent ferments and is required for a few in order to ferment at all. You can purchase temperature controllers preassembled or as a PID controller and temperature probe that require manual wiring.

Measuring in Grams

Yes, here I am, just another cookbook author pleading with you to use a digital gram scale in your kitchen. It will be ever so helpful in creating consistency from batch to batch in your ferments. It will also narrow the possible variables when troubleshooting a ferment gone wrong. Most important, it will give you mad props in any baking circles where you hang out (let alone if you bake bread; the quality of your bread will improve immediately).

If you prefer salting your vegetables to taste, then please continue to do so. If you have been fermenting for years and have a system that works, by all means don't change anything such as adding an amazing digital gram scale to your arsenal. But if you are new to fermentation, even if you swear by your tablespoons and cup measurements in the rest of your kitchen, consider using a gram scale for fermentation due to the ease it provides in calculating salt ratio percentages. With the percentages listed in applicable recipes, you can calculate a repeatable amount of salt every time. You also won't have to worry if your salt is denser than my salt (no, salt is not cut nor created equal).

The recipes in this book are provided in both grams and United States customary units. When accuracy is important, as is the case in baking or weighing some starter cultures, those spoons and cups can create problems. When accuracy is required on a very small scale, even a regular digital gram scale won't cut it. If you're measuring small quantities of ingredients, it is a good idea to have a second gram scale that goes down to a tenth of a gram. The reason to have two scales is because a small one will not be able to weigh a big mixing bowl full of ingredients and a large one will not be sensitive enough to register one-eighth of a teaspoon.

However, even though grams are used throughout this book for consistency and reproducibility, there are many times when I don't use my scale or my measuring spoons. If accuracy is not important beyond flavor, then I will often eyeball the measurement. I love my gram scale, but I'm not married to it.

LIQUID MEASURES

Note that I list even liquid measurements in grams. Although liquid volume is not plagued with the same inaccuracies as dry ingredients (flour, sugar, and salt are some of the worst offenders), I still like to measure liquid with a gram scale so as not to dirty any more utensils or bowls than necessary. My motto when baking is one bowl for all ingredients (unless impossible).

Isn't it fun to explore new ways of approaching old habits? Isn't that, at least in part, why you're reading this book? By no means does fermentation require a scale. If for whatever reason you can't or will not use a scale, that's okay. But I really, really recommend you use one.

Below the Brine

Your mission is to make certain that all fermenting vegetables remain submerged under brine. If you fail, you are at risk of a moldy ferment. If left unchecked, mold could destroy an otherwise delicious fermented food. You have been warned.

There are countless ways to keep your vegetables and fruit below the surface of a salt-water brine. For example, when fermenting cabbage into sauerkraut, I will often use a few cabbage leaves to cover the shredded cabbage in a wide-mouth Mason jar. I then place a 1–2" section of the cabbage core on top of the leaves, which presses and holds the cabbage below the brine once the lid is screwed down.

I call this the "Press and Hold" method. You can also use weights and fingers.

If you do find mold or scum growing on the surface of your ferment, remove any vegetables that were not submerged and skim off any remaining mold. When fermenting vegetables, mold is generally considered safe as long as it is removed. Mold is common enough that it is not something to fear, but if left to grow, it may affect the final texture or flavor of the fermented product.

PRESS AND HOLD METHOD

If you're using a sealed vessel such as a Mason jar with lid, then the Press and Hold method is fine. You will need two objects: one flat item as wide as the Mason jar, and another item as tall as the gap between vegetables and lid.

Flat objects such as full cabbage leaves, slices of beets, ceramic saucers, wooden disks, or plastic lids can work. I especially like to use parts of vegetables because that makes one less thing to wash or clean up once the fermentation process is complete. Any flat object will do as long as it is either small enough to fit inside the mouth of your jar or is flexible enough to bend into place. Food grade and acid tolerant are qualities to consider. Use this flat object (or multiple objects) to cover the soon-to-be-fermenting vegetables.

Next, select another object that will press against the flat object once the lid is sealed. This object should be roughly the length of the distance between lid and vegetables. If the object is too long, then you risk applying too much pressure to the vegetables and forcing brine to overflow the Mason jar.

A cabbage core, a chunk of root vegetable, a wooden dowel, a shot glass, or a small Mason jar will suffice. Press this second object into the flat object, submerging the vegetables in the brine. Screw the Mason jar lid into place. If the vegetables are still not below the brine level, then unscrew the lid and add more brine.

WEIGHT METHOD

If you're using an open vessel such as a ceramic crock, glass jar, food-grade plastic bucket, or wooden barrel, then the weight method will be easy to apply. Any clean object with enough weight to hold the vegetables below the brine level will work.

Options include glass or ceramic weights specifically designed for fermentation, decorative glass beads such as those used in aquariums or flower arrangements, clean stones and rocks, a plastic bag filled with brine, a Mason jar, or a milk jug filled with water.

If the weight you're using does not fully cover the surface of the vegetables, put a plate or other flat object in the vessel first and place the weights on top of the flat object.

Cover the top of the ferment with fabric as protection from dust and flies.

FINGER METHOD

If neither of the previous methods appeals to you, and you are using a sealed container, a third option is to simply monitor your ferments regularly. Opening and checking on your ferments once or twice a day provides opportunity to push down any floating vegetables with clean fingers or a spoon. I often use this method when I wish to taste a vegetable throughout the fermentation process or document the flavor cycle of a new vegetable combination.

Salt Percentages

For vegetable ferments in this book, a salt percentage is listed for each recipe. These percentages correspond to the amount of salt to apply based on the final weight of vegetables to be fermented. If a certain vegetable ferment will produce enough of its own juice, then 2.25% salt is used (listed as "dry"). Wherever a water and salt brine is required, 5% salt is listed (as "brine").

You may notice that the vegetable recipes do not include weight measurements for each vegetable ingredient. Therefore, I've estimated the amount of salt listed in recipes using 2.25% salt based on how many vegetables will fit in the jar. However, if your carrot is larger than my carrot, and if you cram more carrots in than I do, our salt ratios will differ.

The solution is to calculate your own salt instead of following the listed salt ingredient. You can do so by weighing the total amount of vegetables and multiplying it by 0.0225. This will give you the proper amount of salt.

As for vegetables that require a water and salt brine, the percentage is based on the weight of water as opposed to vegetables. If you mix your water and salt based on the ingredients listed, your ratio will be as intended. But if you have fewer vegetables in your jar than I do, you may need more brine. In this case, weighing your additional water and then multiplying that by 0.05 will give you a proper salt brine.

If you don't have an accurate scale, then the amount of salt per recipe will get you close enough to the recommended salt ratio. Given that anywhere between 2–3% works well, you are unlikely to be off by much.

Understanding Temperature

Just as temperature affects humans, it will also affect the microbes in your ferments. Some people function better in, or are acclimated to, warmer climates. If the temperature drops too low, these people may be fussy and unproductive whereas someone acclimated to harsh cold may be actively snowboarding or dogsledding. Yet these same cold-lovers may be drenched in sweat and lethargic if suddenly transported to the tropics. Then there are those humans who are accustomed to large swings in temperature as the seasons change. Such people may do well in any climate as long as they are given some time to adjust.

Most microbes won't die if the temperature fluctuates, but many have ideal temperatures in which they thrive. At the most basic level, when the ambient temperature is cooler, the fermentation process will take longer than when the ambient temperature is warmer. This is very much the case when fermenting vegetables.

However, some microbes won't ferment at all, or unwanted microbes will outcompete them, if they're outside an ideal temperature zone. These different microbes, especially when dealing with cheese and yogurt cultures, are called either mesophilic or thermophilic bacteria. Thermophilic bacteria are heat loving, and this is why making yogurt with thermophilic bacteria requires temperatures near or above 110°F (43°C). Mesophilic bacteria, used in many cheese and heirloom yogurt cultures, won't function properly if incubated at those temperatures. Instead, mesophilic bacteria usually require temperatures at or above room temperature.

Some of the recipes in this book will specify ideal or required temperatures for fermentation. If you don't have a temperature-controlled incubator, it may be useful to explore the temperature ranges of your home. If you have a fully underground basement, then temperatures will remain relatively consistent somewhere in the 50°F–60°F (10°C–16°C) temperature range, which is ideal for many vegetable ferments if you plan to preserve them for many months.

At ground level or above, even if you keep your home's thermostat at a consistent setting, you may be surprised to find how different areas, be they cupboards, closets, hallways, corners, or entire rooms, offer drastically different microclimates for your ferments. If you have access to a thermometer, I recommend placing it, or multiple thermometers, throughout your home in order to catalog potential locations for fermentation. Thermometers that connect via USB can log temperature fluctuation and then upload this data to a computer.

While it's not necessary to own an incubator for most of the fermentation projects throughout this book, having one does remove another variable in the process. The fewer variables, the less chance of something going wrong. Or at least, if something does go wrong, there will be one less variable to rule out (or an easy one to fix) when troubleshooting. I have four temperature-controlled incubators that I use regularly:

FOOD DEHYDRATOR

I will occasionally use my food dehydrator for incubation although the temperature fluctuation is much wider than other options. The main reason I do not use this more often is because it only works for closed-vessel fermentation such as yogurt in a Mason jar. Given that the machine is built to dehydrate food, unless fermenting foods are sealed, they will also dehydrate.

PREASSEMBLED TEMPERATURE CONTROLLER

For a long time my favorite incubator was a preassembled temperature controller often used in home beer making. I primarily use this in a large wooden box, which I insulated with polystyrene. The temperature controller measures the internal temperature of the box and switches an internal 75-watt light bulb on and off in order to maintain a 1°F temperature differential. This style of temperature controller uses an outlet to control a heating device, so I can easily switch between heating devices and incubation chambers.

DIY PID CONTROL

For an even higher degree of accuracy, I use an inexpensive proportional-integral-derivative (PID) controller with a temperature probe and the ability to control both a heating and a cooling device. I use them inside miniature fridges.

For certain ferments that generate their own heat during fermentation such as koji or tempeh, this can be useful. If you place the temperature probe within the fermenting food, the heating element will switch on and off as is normally the case with heat-loving ferments. However, if the fermenting food begins to generate too much heat, then the refrigerator will switch on to cool it to the necessary internal temperature.

Some of the good and inexpensive PID controllers display temperature readings in Celsius only. For this reason, I have included temperature requirements in both Fahrenheit and Celsius for all recipes.

AQUARIUM HEATER AND PUMP

Finally, when ferments such as tempeh or koji require higher levels of humidity, I use a 150-watt submersible aquarium heater in a large plastic tub as an incubator. The heater keeps the water at a consistent temperature, a submersible air pump evens out the heat distribution, and then the water heats a metal pan floating on the surface. The lid is loosely placed on top and the plastic tub is covered with one or more thick blankets.

For as infrequently as the aquarium heater turns on, the water temperature stays surprisingly steady when measured with an external thermometer. The downside to this method is that I need to lug a heavy water-filled container to the bathtub in order to empty and refill it between ferments. One upgrade to this method is to use a large chest cooler on wheels with a spout to empty water.

Timing and Patience

Patience is beyond just a virtue when fermenting; it's a necessity. All fermentation takes time, often more time than other forms of cooking. It may be helpful to begin your fermenting adventure with some of the shorter ferments such as yogurt or soaked grains, which provide near-instant gratification. However, you may also want to jump right in to longer ferments because the sooner you start, the sooner you will finally be able to reap the benefits.

Even foods that ferment for long periods have differing levels of difficulty. Something like sauerkraut takes very little intervention even if fermented for months. However, an aged cheddar cheese will require a few more check-ins before your duties in the fermentation process are fulfilled.

In order to better understand how time affects fermentation, taste your ferments frequently. Try sauerkraut after only a few days and then at least once a week throughout the fermentation process. By doing so, you may surprise yourself with how much you like a younger or older version of one ferment or another. Enjoy the flavors of time through experimentation.

Cultured Funkiness

The perception of flavor, the combination of our sense of smell and taste, is a complex dance of emotion, memory, genetics, and chemistry. It may be impossible for any two people to perceive the same flavor from any one food. The tastes and aromas of food are an amalgamation of our entire existence ensconced in a whiff, slurp, or bite.

That said, it is no wonder that fermented foods can elicit such an array of responses from individuals. If a person from a culture unfamiliar with, and therefore without context for, semi-soft or hard dairy products samples even the most benign and mild cheeses of the western world, she or he may find such food unappetizing if not downright repulsive.

The same can be said for the stinkiest of stinky ferments (fermented fish, anyone?). If, for some reason, you have lived in a bubble your entire life and have never consumed a fermented vegetable, grain, or dairy product, then you may be in for a bit of a shock. Even if you do like some fermented foods, expanding your repertoire and culinary appreciation of others may require a few attempts.

I urge you to step outside of your comfort zone: Test, taste, and sample your way through the many fermented foods in this book and beyond. If you don't like something the first time, circle back to it a few months or years later and you may be surprised by how sophisticated a taster you have become. Your appreciation for food may be forever transformed. As well, a deeper connection with history, culture, and human ingenuity make for an enticing new hobby.

Stick with the stink until the stinky turns funky. Then get ready to boogie with flavors you never dreamed could be so good.

CHAPTER 2

VEGETABLE AND FRUIT FERMENTATION

Fermenting vegetables is one of the easiest processes with which to begin your fermenting journey. We're talking a two-ingredient kind of easy: vegetables and salt. Some vegetables ferment better than others, but all vegetables are edible if left to ferment with a proper amount of salt.

Sometimes salt is introduced in the form of a salt and water brine poured over vegetables. Whereas other times, salt is applied directly to fresh vegetables, and through the process of osmosis, it extracts enough liquid through the cell walls of the vegetables to create the needed salt brine.

This salt brine is the key to most successful vegetable ferments. Some human cultures have fermented vegetables without salt, and a few modern recipes call for using a cultured additive such as whey in order to speed up the process of fermentation and therefore do not require salt. However, the vast majority of fermented vegetables use the protective qualities of salt in order to create an environment that is, at the same time, inhabitable by friendly microbes, and a deterrent to those that would otherwise spoil or contaminate fresh vegetables.

These microorganisms, often in the form of lactic acid bacteria, thrive in higher levels of salinity than is possible for most food spoilage microorganisms. Too much salt will inhibit even the good guys, but not enough salt runs the risk of providing a suitable home for not-so-good bacteria and yeast.

We need to create a comfortable home for the lactic acid bacteria we wish to cultivate. We can do so with the three most accessible variables: time, temperature, and salt. These variables interact with each other in predictable ways. Using sauerkraut as an example, if you prefer mildly sour cabbage, then you will want to ferment your sauerkraut for a shorter period of time, at a cooler temperature, and/or with a higher salt content.

Lower temperatures will slow down the fermentation process. However, too low a temperature will halt fermentation almost completely or encourage the growth of microorganisms that are less inhibited by cold temperatures.

Too much salt will slow fermentation to a crawl (as if microbes could actually crawl), and too little salt will make for an environment that is out of control in regard to which microorganisms will be the most productive. Yet there is no perfect amount of salt for all occasions. If the temperature is low enough, then less salt can be used for similar results compared to higher temperatures and more salt. However, if the temperature is too high, the fermentation process will happen at a much greater speed and may produce off flavors. At a certain point, salt cannot slow down the speed created by heat to a great enough degree without also crossing over a ferment-stopping threshold.

It's up to you to decide which variable to change. In the following vegetable ferments, I specify an amount of salt. I generally use the same amount of salt no matter the temperature; instead I alter the amount of time that I leave my vegetables to ferment in order to control the final product. I do this because I like vegetables with a similar level of salt from batch to batch. With this method, the taste profile changes a bit depending on the temperature when fermenting.

However, if you wish to consume as little salt as possible and you like your ferments on the sour side, you may want to take advantage of fermenting your vegetables in cooler temperatures. You will then be able to use less salt and still ferment for the necessary length of time to build up higher levels of lactic acid. If you do not like a lot of salt but wish to ferment your vegetables in the heat of summer, then you will need to ferment for a very short period of time or use a basement, root cellar, converted refrigerator, or hole in the ground in order to produce temperatures low enough to meet your low salt needs.

A direct way to learn more about the interaction between salt and fermentation is to begin experimenting. The following recipes cover numerous vegetables, styles, and flavors but the outcome will be similar: delicious vegetables for eating and sharing.

Sauerkraut

Sauerkraut is a wonderful ferment for beginners. The reason is simple; it's very difficult to screw up. Chop, salt, and pack the cabbage into a jar; that's it. As long as your cabbage is fresh, it will release plenty of juice by the action of osmosis after salt is applied. Massaging or pounding the cabbage will ensure a breakdown of the cabbage's cellular walls and cause the release of even more juice.

I weigh shredded cabbage and salt nearly every time when making sauerkraut. Anywhere between 2–3% salt to cabbage by weight works well. I use 2.25% salt. If desired, you can use more or less salt in order to balance the time and temperature of your fermenting sauerkraut (see Chapter 1). However, I generally salt at my go-to ratio of 2.25% no matter the ambient temperature or time of year and shorten or extend the overall fermentation period accordingly.

If you're feeling adventurous, you can skip the specific ingredient measurements and instead salt to taste. However, too little salt tends to make for off flavors or texture in sauerkraut. As with all ferments though, one person's bad is another's delicacy, so you may well like mushy and weird-tasting sauerkraut.

Once packed, if your cabbage is not submerged below its own juice brine, there are a few things to consider: Did you massage or pound the cabbage long enough? If not, your cabbage may still be holding on to precious juice. Did you cram the cabbage in tight enough? If not, there may be trapped air or juice pockets that would free up extra space if compressed. Are you using fresh cabbage? If not, your cabbage may have started to dry out, so use a fresher one next time. If you still find your cabbage is not submerged, then make a salt brine by mixing water and 3% salt by weight. Pour this brine into the jar until the cabbage is submerged.

Think of your shredded cabbage as a submarine. Submersion is key. Floating to the surface means exposure to enemy surveillance and attack. In this instance, the enemy is undesirable mold. Remember that the salt brine protects any vegetables below and ensures that desirable bacteria ferment the vegetables as opposed to undesirable microbes rotting them. Keep that cabbage down.

With that said, don't be afraid of moldy cabbage. If you do find mold or scum growing on the top of your brine, scoop it out and your cabbage below will be fine. If any of your cabbage was above the brine and became moldy, then pluck those cabbage shreds and discard them. Any and all cabbage that remains below the brine should still be edible and tasty.

When to call your sauerkraut finished is up to you. Some people like it sweet and short while others like it long and sour. Taste your fermentation projects often in order to define your personal taste and texture preferences. When documenting your favorites, take into consideration that the time of year and temperature will affect the final outcome of your sauerkraut. You may like your sauerkraut best after a week of fermentation in the heat of the summer whereas you may instead like it fermented for a few months come winter. I like to experience my sauerkraut throughout its lifetime (or sometimes I'm simply impatient), and so I taste-test throughout the process.

BASIC SAUERKRAUT

Sauerkraut is in close running with the cucumber pickle as the quintessential fermented vegetable of European descent. Ease of fermentation is one feature where cabbage undoubtedly trumps cucumbers. It may take a few attempts to master, but once you've got the hang of it sauerkraut is really tough to screw up.

Once you deem your sauerkraut complete, store it in a refrigerator to halt the fermentation process. Instead of refrigeration, you can also store your finished sauerkraut in a basement or root cellar with the caveat that the sauerkraut will continue to ferment and sour slowly over extended periods of time.

YIELD: 1 QUART

🕐 **PREP:** 20 minutes

🫙 **FERMENTATION:** 3 days–6 months

🧂 **SALT:** 2.25% dry

900 grams (2 pounds) cabbage

20 grams (2 tablespoons) salt

1. Remove outer leaves of cabbage and save them.

2. Slice cabbage into quarters, remove core, and save core.

3. Shred cabbage.

4. In a bowl, combine shredded cabbage and salt.

5. Massage cabbage until soft and juicy, from 2–15 minutes.

6. Pack cabbage and juice into a quart-size jar. Make certain the cabbage is submerged below the brine of cabbage juice. Apply added pressure to the cabbage while packing in order to ensure there are no trapped air pockets in the jar.

7. Leave at least 1" of space between lip of jar and brine.

8. Cover the shredded cabbage with a layer or two of cabbage leaves. Then place a chunk of cabbage core on top of the cabbage leaves.

9. Close lid of jar and make certain that the cabbage core is holding the shredded cabbage below the brine.

10. Leave to ferment, away from direct sunlight, for as little as 3 days or up to 6 months.

11. Make certain to release any CO_2 buildup in the first week by quickly opening and closing the lid.

12. When fermentation is to your liking, move to long-term storage (i.e., refrigerator, basement, root cellar).

PRETTY IN PINK

Unless you use red cabbage, your sauerkraut shouldn't be pink. If it is, you probably used too much salt, causing certain microbes to impart the pink color. No harm done except to flavor and texture. Use less salt next time.

JUNIPER BERRY SAUERKRAUT

Adding spices and other vegetables to sauerkraut offers complexity to an otherwise simple ferment. This can be especially important if you start making a lot of sauerkraut and crave variety. For a traditional and old-world style, consider adding caraway seeds and juniper berries.

I recommend adding juniper berries to the top of the ferment as opposed to mixing them in with the cabbage and caraway seeds. I love the flavor that juniper berries impart throughout the sauerkraut, but I do not particularly like biting into the fermented berries themselves. They have an overpowering flavor (far different from the fresh or dried berry). When I add them to the top of the jar, they are easy to scoop out once fermentation is complete.

900 grams (2 pounds) cabbage, shredded

20 grams (2 tablespoons) salt

7 grams (1 tablespoon) caraway seeds

10 grams (2 tablespoons) juniper berries

1. In a bowl, combine cabbage, salt, and caraway seeds.

2. Massage cabbage until soft and juicy, from 2–15 minutes.

3. Pack cabbage and juice into a quart-size jar making certain the cabbage is submerged below the brine of cabbage juice.

4. Leave at least 1" of space between lip of jar and brine.

5. Add juniper berries to top of jar.

6. Cover juniper berries and cabbage with a layer of cabbage leaves. Then place a chunk of cabbage core on top of the cabbage leaves.

7. Close lid of jar and make certain that the cabbage core is holding the shredded cabbage below the brine.

8. Leave to ferment, away from direct sunlight, for as little as 1 week or up to 6 months.

9. Make certain to release any CO_2 buildup in the first week by quickly opening and closing the lid.

10. When fermentation is to your liking, move to long-term storage (i.e., refrigerator, basement, root cellar).

YIELD: 1 QUART

- **PREP:** 20 minutes
- **FERMENTATION:** 1 week–2 months
- **SALT:** 2.25% dry

SPICY SAUERKRAUT

Once you've tried a few simple versions of sauerkraut, you can begin exploring the endless flavor combinations available to you. These sauerkrauts begin to blur the lines between sauerkraut, kimchi, and other fermented vegetables, but in my heart, I still consider them sauerkrauts because the base ingredient is regular European-style cabbage.

Try the following recipe and then begin to create your own combinations. You can find inspiration anywhere from a nonfermented coleslaw recipe to the ingredients list of relishes and chutneys available in the grocery store. Go completely wild and mix up your entire spice cabinet and vegetable drawer (or garden) for a "suicide" sauerkraut.

350 grams (1 pound) cabbage, shredded

1 large carrot, julienned

1 medium onion, chopped

1 medium red bell pepper, julienned

1 large jalapeño, seeds removed, and chopped

20 grams (2 tablespoons) salt

10 grams (1 tablespoon) mustard seed

1. In a bowl, combine cabbage, carrot, onion, bell pepper, jalapeño, salt, and mustard seed.

2. Massage until vegetables are soft and juicy, from 2–15 minutes.

3. Pack vegetables and juice into a quart-size jar making certain the vegetables are submerged below the brine of cabbage juice.

4. Leave at least 1" of space between lip of jar and brine.

5. Cover vegetables with a layer of cabbage leaves. Then place a chunk of cabbage core on top of the cabbage leaves.

6. Close lid of jar and make certain that the cabbage core is holding the vegetables below the brine.

7. Leave to ferment, away from direct sunlight, for as little as 1 week or up to 2 months.

8. Make certain to release any CO_2 buildup in the first week by quickly opening and closing the lid.

9. When fermentation is to your liking, move to long-term storage (i.e., refrigerator, basement, root cellar).

CHAPTER 2: **Vegetable and Fruit Fermentation**   41

🕐 **PREP:** 10 minutes

🫙 **FERMENTATION:** 2–6 months

🧂 **SALT:** 5% brine

SOUR BRUSSELS SPROUTS

These things stink and taste weird in the first few weeks of fermentation. Eventually though, you will be rewarded. Even if you don't like Brussels sprouts, fermented ones may change your mind. But please don't jump the gun; wait to taste these bundles of joy until they are ready.

When fermented for extended periods of time, they remain firmer than sauerkraut, and I think of them as little disks of crunchy sourness. They taste different than sauerkraut too. Alone they are delicious, but they really shine as an ingredient in stir fry, pizza, and noodle dishes.

200 grams (½ pound) Brussels sprouts, halved

350 grams (1½ cups) water

17 grams (1½ tablespoons) salt

1. Pack the Brussels sprouts into a glass jar.

2. Mix water and salt in a separate jar or bowl until dissolved.

3. Pour salt-water brine over Brussels sprouts until submerged.

4. Weigh down Brussels sprouts below brine and close lid.

5. Leave at room temperature, away from direct sunlight, for 2–6 months.

6. Make certain to release any CO_2 buildup in the first week by quickly opening and closing the lid.

7. When fermentation is to your liking, move to long-term storage (i.e., refrigerator, basement, root cellar).

NAMING FERMENTS

Once you begin fermenting nontraditional vegetable combinations, there may be no existing categories or names for your creations. Author and fermentation revivalist Sandor Katz puts these hybrid vegetable ferments under the category of "kraut-chi."

Kimchi

Kimchi has a long tradition in Korean cuisine and is the national dish of South Korea. Using seasonal and traditional ingredients available in differing regions, kimchi has developed many different forms. Quick ferments may be ready within hours or days and aged ferments can provide for families throughout long winters. There are sweet kimchis, spicy kimchis, and all kimchis in between.

Having only visited Seoul, South Korea, during an extended airport layover, I make no claim that the following kimchi recipes are traditional or authentic. They are inspired by Korean cuisine and flavors but some of the methods or final outcomes are different.

For example, it is often customary to coat cabbage with a high proportion of salt and leave it to sit for many hours. This process leaches water from the cabbage and slowly breaks down plant cell walls. I prefer to do the same thing with my hands. Massaging cabbage and other vegetables, in the same way as I do for sauerkraut, allows me to speed up the process without degrading quality or flavor. It may not be proper kimchi form, but it works.

After reading through and attempting one or more of the following kimchi recipes, experiment with your own ingredient combinations.

RED KIMCHI

This is the first style of kimchi with which I fell in love, and it remains high on my list of all-time favorite fermented foods. Hot, spicy, and refreshing. These flavors meld into something greater than themselves during fermentation. Do not forget the fish sauce. It provides an extra punch of umami and really rounds out the taste experience.

1 large napa cabbage, cut into 1" chunks

3 carrots, julienned

1 small daikon radish, julienned

1 bunch green onions, julienned

50 grams (4 tablespoons) salt

1 ginger chunk (1–2" in length), peeled

3 cloves garlic

1 apple or pear

20 grams (2 tablespoons) Korean coarse red pepper

14 grams (1 tablespoon) fish sauce

1. Mix the cabbage, carrots, daikon radish, green onions, and salt in a bowl.

2. Using a food processor, blender, or pestle and mortar, puree the ginger, garlic, apple (or pear), red pepper, and fish sauce into a paste.

3. Mix the paste with the vegetables.

4. Pack the vegetables and paste into 1 or more glass jars.

5. Ensure that the vegetables remain below the brine.

6. Leave to ferment, away from direct sunlight, for 1–2 weeks and then transfer to the refrigerator.

NOT ALL PEPPER FLAKES ARE CREATED EQUAL

Explore the Asian grocery stores in your area to find Korean coarse red pepper powder. The peppers and the drying process are different than most peppers, and the taste is distinctive. Make sure it's made in Korea too; the price difference is worth it.

BRUSSELS SPROUT KIMCHI

Imagine the taste of kimchi translated into bite-size cabbages. The flavors of ginger, green onion, garlic, red pepper, and fish sauce mingle with these half orbs in a tantalizing fashion. This recipe is similar in taste profile to the Red Kimchi recipe; the main difference is that the vegetables are diced.

Also note the use of banana. You can substitute an apple, pear, or sugar, but I sometimes use a banana as sweetener when I have no other fruit available.

200 grams (½ pound) Brussels sprouts, halved

2 large carrots, diced

1 leek, diced

1" piece of ginger, peeled

2 cloves garlic

1 banana

10 grams (1 tablespoon) crushed red pepper or powder

6 grams (1 teaspoon) fish sauce

25 grams (1½ tablespoons) salt

500 grams (2 cups) water

1. Place the Brussels sprouts, carrots, and leek into a bowl.

2. Using a food processor, blender, or pestle and mortar, puree the ginger, garlic, banana, red pepper, and fish sauce into a paste.

3. Mix the paste in with the other ingredients.

4. Pack the vegetables and paste into a quart-size jar.

5. Prepare salt brine by mixing salt and water in a separate jar.

6. Pour enough brine over vegetables until submerged.

7. Ensure that the vegetables remain below the brine.

8. Leave to ferment, away from direct sunlight, for 1–2 weeks and then transfer to the refrigerator.

PREP: 15 minutes

FERMENTATION: 1–4 weeks

SALT: 2.25% dry

BLANKIMCHI

This is my plain version of so-called kimchi, or as I like to say, my blankimchi. It contains only napa cabbage and carrots fermented for 1 month. To obtain the effervescent texture, this recipe is fermented at room temperature for the first week and then allowed to slowly carbonate in the refrigerator for the last 3 weeks. If you do not desire bubbles, then this blankimchi can be opened and used anytime after the first week.

1 large head napa cabbage, chopped

3 large carrots, julienned

35 grams (2½ tablespoons) salt

1. Combine cabbage, carrots, and salt in a large bowl.

2. Massage cabbage to release cabbage juice.

3. Pack the vegetables and any juice from bowl into a half-gallon Mason jar or other fermentation vessel. The vegetables should be submerged below the cabbage juice.

4. Allow vegetables to ferment for 1 week at room temperature.

5. Refrigerate jar and allow to ferment slowly for 3 additional weeks before use.

KIMCHI CRISIS

In the fall of 2010, there was a "kimchi crisis" that resulted in South Koreans paying extremely high prices for napa cabbage, or going without, due to abnormal weather and a resulting cabbage shortage. For a society that eats kimchi with nearly every meal, this was serious.

Other Fruit and Vegetable Ferments

Although the following recipes are not sauerkraut or kimchi, most of them are similar in preparation and technique. The process of fermenting vegetables in salt is universal, and the same concepts can be applied to any vegetables available to you.

Fruit is a little more challenging because of the high sugar content in many fruits. This sugar is begging for yeast to ferment it into alcohol, which generally is not the desired result when making fruit and vegetable ferments like these. Unless you use a lot of salt, fermented fruits will turn to alcohol. However, fruits can be added to vegetable mixtures much the same way apples and bananas were added to the kimchi recipes.

The one drastically different fermentation method that easily could have an entire section devoted to it is nukazuke. This Japanese style of ferment uses moist rice bran as a fermentation medium as opposed to brine. Instead of vegetables taking weeks to ferment, once a nuka pot is mature and established, vegetables can be ready within only a few hours or days.

SPICY DILL CARROTS

Some of the sweetness remains in these carrots after fermentation and this pairs well with the overall sour and spicy flavors. Makes an excellent snack, side dish, or ingredient.

5 large carrots, sliced in quarters

2 sprigs fresh dill

2 cloves garlic, sliced

5 grams (½ tablespoon) red pepper flakes

750 grams (3 cups) water

38 grams (2 tablespoons) salt

1. Pack carrots, dill, garlic, and red pepper flakes into a quart-size jar.

2. Mix salt-water brine in a separate jar or bowl.

3. Fill jar with salt brine until all carrots are submerged. Prepare more brine if necessary.

4. Weigh down the carrots so that they remain below the brine.

5. Close lid on jar and leave to ferment, away from direct sunlight, for 2–4 weeks.

6. Make certain to release any CO_2 buildup in the first week by quickly opening and closing the lid.

7. When fermentation is to your liking, move to long-term storage (i.e., refrigerator, basement, root cellar).

🕐 **PREP:** 10 minutes

🫙 **FERMENTATION:** 2–4 weeks

🧂 **SALT:** 5% brine

DILL GREEN BEANS

If you ferment no other recipe in this book, please try these dill green beans. I enjoy dill pickles, but I *love* dill green beans. Compared to cucumber pickles, a crunchy end product is much easier to achieve. For an added kick, add fresh or crushed red pepper.

900 grams (2 pounds) green beans, ends trimmed

2–4 sprigs fresh dill

4 cloves garlic, sliced

1500 grams (6 cups) water

75 grams (3½ tablespoons) salt

1. Pack green beans, dill, and garlic into 2 quart-size jars.

2. Mix salt-water brine in a separate jar or bowl.

3. Fill jars with salt brine until all green beans are submerged. Prepare more brine if necessary.

4. Weigh down the beans so that they remain below the brine.

5. Close lid on jar and leave to ferment, away from direct sunlight, for 2–4 weeks.

6. Make certain to release any CO_2 buildup in the first week by quickly opening and closing the lid.

7. When fermentation is to your liking, move to long-term storage (i.e., refrigerator, basement, root cellar).

Silly Dilly

Fermented or canned, this style of green beans is often referred to as "dilly," but I've never liked that term. No hard feelings if you have fond memories associated with the name. It is not that I mind a silly word like "dilly," but these green beans taste far more sophisticated and delicious than "dilly" could ever portray.

YIELD: 1 QUART

⏱ **PREP:** 10 minutes

🫙 **FERMENTATION:** 3–6 weeks

🧂 **SALT:** 5% brine

LEEK RINGS

A simple, yet elegant, example of how easy fermentation can be. Experience the transformation by sampling the leeks pre- and post-fermentation. Leeks, salt, and thyme aren't really that exciting when mixed fresh. But after a few weeks and once lactic acid bacteria have done their thing, this recipe turns sour, the leeks mellow out and become tender, and the thyme fully infuses the rings. This goes especially well with goat cheese on a toasted cracker.

4 large leeks, sliced into ¼" rounds

700 grams (3 cups) water

35 grams (2½ tablespoons) salt

8 grams (2 tablespoons) thyme

1. Gently transfer the leeks to a quart-size jar while attempting to keep most of the inner rings intact.

2. Combine the water, salt, and thyme in a separate jar or bowl until the salt dissolves.

3. Pour the salt brine over the leeks until submerged.

4. Weighing down the leeks below the brine is optional but not necessary if checked regularly.

5. Leave to ferment, away from direct sunlight, for at least 3 weeks until leeks are tender.

6. Make certain to release any CO_2 buildup in the first week by quickly opening and closing the lid.

7. When fermentation is to your liking, move to long-term storage (i.e., refrigerator, basement, root cellar).

FERMENTED RED ONIONS

I absolutely do not like the taste of raw onions, and I especially loathe the awfulness that lingers in my mouth hours after eating them. The smell of someone else's onion breath is even worse! However, I love the taste of cooked onions. Not too surprisingly, I also love the taste of fermented red onions. These fermented onions give off a sweeter taste and aroma as if they were cooked but the major bonus is that they only retain a slight pungency. They are enjoyable and remain crisp and crunchy. If stored in the refrigerator, your fermented onions should last anywhere from 6 months to 1 year. Note that after a few months, they are still edible despite their dull and faded appearance.

4 large red onions, chopped or diced

1500 grams (6 cups) water

35 grams (2 tablespoons) salt

1. Pack red onions into 1 half-gallon or 2 quart-size jars.

2. Combine water and salt in a separate bowl or jar.

3. Fill jar with salt brine until onions are submerged. Prepare more brine if necessary.

4. Close lid on jar and leave to ferment, away from direct sunlight, for 2–4 weeks.

5. Make certain to release any CO_2 buildup in the first week by quickly opening and closing the lid.

6. When fermentation is to your liking, move to long-term storage (i.e., refrigerator, basement, root cellar).

WHAT ABOUT ONION BREATH?

I haven't made anyone smell my breath after consuming these fermented onions, but I can say that the lingering aftertaste is nowhere near as strong as fresh raw onions. An aftertaste still exists, but I can eat a spoonful or two of these fermented onions without disgust.

SWEET LEEK MEDLEY

Beets are so sweet that not even fermentation can sour them. Or so goes the taste profile of this leek and beet ferment. They will, however, become more sour and less sweet the longer they are fermented. These fermented vegetables work well tossed in pasta or served with rice.

1 large leek, diced

1 medium beet, diced

2 medium carrots, julienned

750 grams (3 cups) water

38 grams (2 tablespoons) salt

1. Pack leek, beet, and carrots into a quart-size jar.

2. Mix salt-water brine in a separate jar or bowl.

3. Fill jar with salt brine until all vegetables are submerged. Prepare more brine if necessary.

4. Weigh vegetables down so that they remain below the brine.

5. Close lid on jar and leave to ferment, away from direct sunlight, for 2 weeks to 4 months.

6. Make certain to release any CO_2 buildup in the first week by quickly opening and closing the lid.

7. When fermentation is to your liking, move to long-term storage (i.e., refrigerator, basement, root cellar).

GIARDINIERA

I was amazed the first time I tried fermenting cauliflower. It is one of my favorite fermented vegetables and doesn't get enough love in most home kitchens. Ferment cauliflower alone or try this vegetable mix. Use it to make a Muffuletta Sandwich (see Chapter 10) or add it to pasta. Like it spicy? Add as many hot peppers as you can handle.

1 head cauliflower, chopped

2 large carrots, julienned

1 zucchini, sliced

3 cloves garlic, diced

750 grams (3 cups) water

38 grams (2 tablespoons) salt

1. Pack cauliflower, carrots, zucchini, and garlic into a quart-size jar.

2. Mix salt-water brine in a separate jar or bowl.

3. Fill jar with salt brine until all vegetables are submerged. Prepare more brine if necessary.

4. Weigh down vegetables so that they remain below the brine.

5. Close lid on jar and leave to ferment, away from direct sunlight, for 2–6 weeks.

6. Make certain to release any CO_2 buildup in the first week by quickly opening and closing the lid.

7. When fermentation is to your liking, move to long-term storage (i.e., refrigerator, basement, root cellar).

SOUR WATERMELON RINDS

Sometimes, a special kind of joy comes from fermenting a food item that would otherwise go unused. Watermelon rinds are a great example of this. They are edible, but most people discard them. These rinds get a second chance once fermented in a salt brine. Simple and effective, these rinds are mild and sour when fermented alone. This makes them a blank canvas for your favorite sour pairings. Dill rinds, anyone? If you choose to keep them plain, they are an excellent addition to yogurt-based pasta sauces.

Rind of watermelon, cubed or sliced, ½" thick

750 grams (3 cups) water

38 grams (2 tablespoons) salt

1. Pack rinds into a quart-size jar.

2. Combine salt-water brine in a separate jar or bowl.

3. Fill jar with salt brine until all rinds are submerged. Prepare more brine if necessary.

4. Weigh down rinds so that they remain below the brine.

5. Close lid on jar and leave to ferment, away from direct sunlight, for 1–4 weeks.

6. Make certain to release any CO_2 buildup in the first week by quickly opening and closing the lid.

7. When fermentation is to your liking, move to long-term storage (i.e., refrigerator, basement, root cellar).

🕐 **PREP:** 5 minutes

🫙 **FERMENTATION:** 4–6 weeks

PRESERVED LEMONS

The real magic of preserved lemons is in the rind. The rind transforms into a tender and sweet, almost candy-like, ingredient that can be used in any recipe that calls for lemon zest or juice. It adds a mouthful of umami flavor too. Use the juice and pulp for dressings and marinades.

Weight or volume measurements are not necessary for this ferment. These lemons are used as an ingredient in cooking, often replacing salt, and are not generally eaten alone. Don't be afraid of salting these lemons too much. As much as they can hold is as much as they need. However, do not add extra salt to the brine or jar.

4–5 lemons, partially quartered and stems removed

Sea or kosher salt

Lemon juice

1. Place each lemon in a bowl, cut side up, and fill with salt until overflowing. Once all lemons are salted, pack them into a quart-size jar, pressing firmly down. Close lid and leave at room temperature for 24 hours.

2. Salt will have leached lemon juice from the lemons, and the juice will have collected at the bottom of the jar. Open jar and firmly press down the lemons.

3. Add enough lemon juice to submerge the lemons. Close lid and leave at room temperature for 2–3 days. Shake the jar daily to redistribute the salt and, if necessary, remove lid and press lemons below the lemon juice brine.

4. Leave to ferment, away from direct sunlight, for 4–6 weeks. Move to a cool basement or refrigerator until ready to use. Unopened, these lemons will last 6 months to 1 year although they will darken in color.

Not Enough Lemons for Juice?

Preserved lemons can also be made using a salt-water brine instead of a salt-lemon brine. Flavor will be slightly diluted, but the fermentation process is the same. Instead of adding lemon juice in the final steps, add water.

PREP: 30 minutes + 1 minute daily

FERMENTATION: 2 weeks

NUKAZUKE

Before you can make rice bran pickles, you first need to prepare rice bran in a crock or similar vessel. After a few weeks your rice bran nuka pot will be mature enough to begin fermenting vegetables. The true beauty of the nuka pot is that once it's established, vegetables can be soured and fermented in less than a day (although at first it may take a few days). If you start a nuka pot, you will need to stir it every single day. Treat your nuka "pet" well.

910 grams (8 cups) bran, rice or wheat

350 grams (1½ cups) beer

350 grams (1½ cups) water

200 grams (¾ cup) salt

Apple skins from 2 apples, sliced

4 cabbage leaves, whole

35 grams (about 2½") ginger, sliced

1. Toast bran over medium heat until lightly browned and aromatic. Stir constantly to prevent burning.

2. Remove from heat and allow to cool.

3. Combine toasted bran, beer, water, and salt in a large crock. Stir by hand until thoroughly mixed. The bran mixture should feel like wet sand. Add more water if necessary but do not overwater.

4. Bury apple skins, cabbage leaves, and ginger in the rice bran mixture. Gently press down on the top of the rice bran. Wipe debris from exposed sides and edges. Cover with a cloth and leave to ferment for 1 week.

5. After the first week, stir the nuka pot at least once a day by hand, making certain to cover with cloth after each use.

6. After the second week, remove apple skins, cabbage leaves, and ginger from the nuka pot. You may find forgotten pieces of fruit or vegetable during daily stirring by hand and you can simply remove them at that time.

7. When ready to begin fermenting vegetables in the nuka pot, first wash and rub salt on the outside of vegetables. Then bury vegetables in the nuka pot and leave to ferment for a few hours and up to a few weeks. The nuka pot will be slow to ferment at first, but after a few weeks should begin to sour vegetables within 1 day.

8. Continue to ferment new vegetables and to stir daily for the rest of your life (or the life of the nuka pot).

CHAPTER 3

DAIRY FERMENTATION

Cows are large animals and they produce a lot of milk. Throughout history, the milk of cows, goats, sheep, and horses have been transformed through fermentation in order to preserve abundant supplies of this nutrient-rich substance.

Before the advent of pasteurization and refrigeration, milk would naturally sour at ambient temperatures. Lactic acid bacteria are present in raw milk, and the fermentation process keeps milk from contaminating. While this natural souring process will prolong the shelf life of milk for a few days, other methods were developed to extend the storability of milk.

Fermented beverages such as kefir and foods such as yogurt and cheese have long been staples in dairy-consuming cultures around the world. While there are advanced techniques involved in some forms of cheese making, most dairy ferments are easy to make at home.

The recipes in this chapter have been created using pasteurized whole cow's milk, unless otherwise noted. If you choose to use lower fat milk, your results will vary in regard to thickness and texture of the final product.

If you plan to use unpasteurized, or raw, milk, then it will be important to also keep a small batch of pasteurized culture in order to maintain consistency and vitality of your starter cultures. Otherwise, the native microbes in your raw milk may outcompete and destroy the cultures you wish to cultivate.

Heirloom Yogurt

All yogurts were once heirloom yogurts and so this terminology is relatively new. The term "heirloom" refers to the fact that, if properly cared for, a yogurt culture can be used to inoculate future batches of yogurt, therefore perpetuating the flavor profile and texture of a specific dairy ferment indefinitely.

This differs from direct-set yogurt starter cultures, which are comprised of laboratory-derived strains of bacteria used to inoculate milk. Direct-set starter cultures are not meant to be reused, or backslopped, as dairy ferments have been throughout history.

Consistency is important in commercial production, but at home you can obtain and use heirloom yogurt cultures so you don't have to repurchase starter cultures regularly in order to make yogurt.

All of the dairy cultures in this section can be purchased online (see Appendix) but also check locally to see if anyone in your area has cultures to share. Once you have obtained cultures, be sure to pass them along to your friends and family.

BULGARIAN YOGURT

Bulgarian yogurt was the sample yogurt used when, in the early 1900s, microbiologists isolated specific thermophilic, or heat-loving, bacteria (*Lactobacillus delbrueckii* subsp. *bulgaricus* and *Streptococcus thermophilus*), to which the flavor and texture of yogurt were then attributed. Thus began the use of direct-set starter cultures in the production of commercial yogurt.

Heirloom Bulgarian yogurt can be perpetuated indefinitely. You can also use commercial yogurt as a starter but you may find you need to start over with a fresh yogurt sample after a few backslopped generations because milk no longer ferments correctly.

The heating process denatures milk proteins, causing the final yogurt to be thicker when the proteins bond together again. If you would like to make a thinner, or drinkable, yogurt, you can skip preheating the milk.

950 grams (1 quart) whole milk

15 grams (2 tablespoons) Bulgarian yogurt

1. Pour milk into a quart-size jar but do not close the lid.

2. Place a towel in the bottom of a pot and place the jar of milk in the pot. Fill the pot with water so that the jar is nearly surrounded by water.

3. Place a thermometer probe in the milk and heat the pot on medium low until the internal temperature of the milk reaches 165°F (74°C). Either turn off the heat at this time, or continue to hold at this temperature for up to 30 minutes. The longer the milk heats, the thicker the resulting yogurt will be due to evaporation. Alternatively, heat the milk directly in a pot and transfer to a jar when ready to inoculate. Do not heat above 180°F (82°C).

4. Loosely attach the lid to the jar and allow the milk to cool to 115°F (46°C). This can be accomplished by submerging the pot in ice-cold water (do not directly submerge the jar while still hot to avoid breaking the glass) or by removing the jar from the pot and allowing to cool at room temperature.

5. Once cooled, inoculate the milk with Bulgarian yogurt or Bulgarian yogurt starter. Seal with lid and shake gently to combine.

6. Leave to ferment in a very warm spot or in an incubator at 110°F (43°C) for 6–12 hours, or until yogurt has thickened. Test by tilting jar. If yogurt pulls away cleanly from side, then yogurt is ready.

7. Before opening jar, refrigerate yogurt until fully cold.

8. Before consuming, scoop out enough yogurt for making future batches and refrigerate in a small sealed jar. The strongest selection of microbes will come from all areas of the jar, so scoop deep into the center.

9. Repeat process at least once a week to maintain a healthy Bulgarian yogurt culture.

MATSONI

Also known as Caspian Sea yogurt, this mesophilic yogurt comes from the region now known as Georgia, or possibly Armenia, and may be thick and ropy or thin and lumpy depending on the starter culture obtained. There has been some divergence of this yogurt as it has spread across the world, and so the defining characteristics are somewhat vague. It is safe to say that this is a mild and pleasant-tasting yogurt.

950 grams (1 quart) whole milk

23 grams (3 tablespoons) matsoni yogurt

1. Combine milk and yogurt in a quart-size jar. Seal with lid and shake gently to combine.

2. Leave to ferment at room temperature for 12–24 hours (ideal temperatures range from 69°F–89°F (35°C–44°C), or until yogurt has thickened. Test by tilting jar. If yogurt pulls away cleanly from side, or doesn't tilt at all, then matsoni is ready.

3. Before opening jar, refrigerate until fully cold.

4. Before consuming, scoop out enough matsoni for making future batches and store in refrigerator in a small sealed jar. The strongest selection of microbes will come from all areas of the jar, so scoop deep into the center.

5. Repeat process at least once a week to maintain a healthy matsoni culture.

STRAINED YOGURT

Removing excess liquid from yogurt makes for a much thicker finished product often referred to as yogurt cheese, labneh, or Greek yogurt. The longer it strains, the thicker it will become. This thick yogurt can be enjoyed as is or in spreads, dips, and desserts.

2000 grams (8 cups) thermophilic yogurt (Bulgarian heirloom yogurt or plain store-bought yogurt)

6 grams (½ teaspoon) salt (optional)

1. Combine yogurt and salt in a bowl. Note: Omit salt if making Greek yogurt as opposed to yogurt cheese.

2. Line another large bowl with fine-mesh cheesecloth or muslin and pour the yogurt into the cheesecloth. Pull up all 4 corners of the cheesecloth and tie them together. Whey will begin to drip into the bowl.

3. Hang yogurt and cheesecloth from sink faucet, a hook installed under cabinets, or by other means. Keep bowl underneath to capture dripping whey. If planning to use whey for other projects, empty from bowl at least every 2 hours and refrigerate whey.

4. Leave to strain for 6 hours if making Greek yogurt. Strain for up to 24 hours if making yogurt cheese or labneh.

5. Remove from cheesecloth and store strained yogurt in refrigerator or roll into balls and store in olive oil.

It's All Greek to Me

"Greek" is like the "Kleenex" of strained yogurts. Most of the Greek yogurt sold in the United States is not made in Greece. Many cultures have strained yogurt throughout history, but Greece has taken hold as the origin of this thick yogurt, at least in U.S. marketing usage.

KEFIR

Kefir (pronounced kay-fear or key-fur) is believed to have originated in the Caucasus Mountains. While some commercial companies have begun using laboratory-derived starter cultures for kefir production, the most common home method remains the traditional use of kefir grains. Kefir grains are a symbiotic colony of bacteria and yeast, which are used to inoculate fresh milk and produce a mildly sour and yeast-flavored beverage. Instead of backslopping, as is the case with heirloom yogurt, the kefir grains are strained from each batch of fermented milk and reused for subsequent batches. The grains will continue to multiply over time and can be shared, eaten, or used to make larger batches of kefir.

PREP: 5 minutes

FERMENTATION:
12–24 hours

850 grams (3½ cups) whole milk

10–20 grams (1–2 tablespoons) kefir grains

1. Combine milk and kefir grains in a quart-size jar. Close lid and leave to ferment for 12–24 hours.

2. If the milk solids and whey begin to separate during fermentation, shake the jar to recombine. This is similar to how, when kefir was once fermented in animal-skin bags, visitors to a home in the Caucasus Mountains were obliged to kick the kefir bag that hung next to the door before exiting.

3. Once milk thickens, turns bubbly, and smells faintly of yeast, strain the newly fermented kefir through a sieve in order to retrieve the kefir grains. Alternatively, if your grains are large enough, scoop them out with a fork or other utensil.

4. Use the grains immediately to make a fresh batch of kefir or store them in the refrigerator with a small portion of milk until ready to use.

5. Fresh kefir can be consumed immediately, stored in the refrigerator, or allowed to ferment in a closed container for 1 or more days for a more sour and carbonated beverage.

MULTIPLYING GRAINS

Your kefir grains will grow in size and/or number over time, but the speed at which they grow is dependent on multiple factors including environment and your specific grains. Remove some of these grains if your kefir begins to over-ferment.

VIILI

Of all the heirloom yogurts that I keep, viili is one of my favorites. Viili is thought to have originated in Finland (or that general region). Both ropy and non-ropy cultures (a.k.a. long and short) are available online. However, if you want true enjoyment, it is important to obtain a viili culture with a ropy, or stringy, consistency that stretches like honey. GEM Cultures (see Appendix) maintains one of the oldest viili cultures in the United States.

My first experience was with short viili. It was okay but not drastically different from other heirloom yogurts that I had tried. However, once I experienced long viili, I was hooked. It is mesmerizing the way it stretches and slides across a spoon with a similarly tantalizing movement across the tongue. For beginners, there may be a slight challenge to getting the thick goo from bowl to mouth, but it is a welcome change from the average yogurt that is so easy to shovel onto your tongue.

250 grams (1 cup) whole milk

10 grams (2 teaspoons) viili culture

1. With the back of a spoon, rub and coat viili culture along the inside edges and bottom of a small bowl.

2. Pour milk into the bowl.

3. Cover the bowl with a small plate or towel.

4. Leave to ferment at room temperature for 12–24 hours, or until viili has set up like gelatin and stretches when lifted with a spoon.

5. Save enough fresh viili for future batches.

6. Repeat process at least once a week to maintain a viable viili culture.

Stretch That Yogurt

The texture of long viili comes from the polysaccharide bonds formed by lactic acid bacteria. The primary bacteria responsible for the slime are classified as *Lactococcus lactis* subsp. *cremoris*. These bacteria are also prevalent in kefir, but in that case the polysaccharide matrix forms into grains instead of a slimy yogurt.

YIELD: 1 QUART

🕐 **PREP:** 2 minutes

🫙 **FERMENTATION:** 12–24 hours

PIIMÄ AND FILMJÖLK

Like viili, piimä and filmjölk are Scandinavian mesophilic fermented dairy products. Piimä is much thinner and drinkable with a mild and almost nutty flavor. Piimä works great as a buttermilk substitute.

Filmjölk, also referred to as "fil," has a distinct, yet mild, butter or cheese flavor. This flavor and aroma are derived from diacetyl-producing bacteria (mainly *Lactococcus lactis* subsp. *lactis* biovar *diacetylactis*). Filmjölk is thicker than piimä but is still drinkable.

Both piimä and filmjölk can be prepared in the same way.

950 grams (1 quart) whole milk

15 grams (2 tablespoons) piimä or filmjölk yogurt

1. Combine milk and yogurt in a quart-size jar. Seal with lid and shake gently to combine.

2. Leave to ferment at room temperature for 12–24 hours. (Ideal temperatures range from 70°F–80°F (21°C–26°C), or until yogurt has thickened. Test by tilting jar. If yogurt pulls away cleanly from side, then yogurt is ready. Note: Piimä will be thinner than filmjölk.

3. Before opening jar, refrigerate yogurt until fully cold.

4. Before consuming, scoop out enough piimä or filmjölk for making future batches and store in refrigerator in a small sealed jar. The strongest selection of microbes will come from all areas of the jar, so scoop deep into the center.

5. Repeat process at least once a week to maintain a healthy piimä or filmjölk culture.

Cultured Whipped Cream

You can culture cream just as easily as milk. If you've already begun making your own mesophilic yogurts, then you already have the necessary starter culture to make cultured butter and cultured whipped cream. The fermentation process is the same as for yogurt, but both whipped cream and butter require extra steps for the final product. However, cultured cream is delicious without alteration too. Enjoy it as a thick substitute to yogurt.

CULTURED BUTTER

Cultured butter is better. It is more complex in flavor compared to sweet cream butter. Making it yourself is less expensive than specialty store varieties. Even if the flavor is complex, there is nothing complicated or difficult about making it; all it requires is a little muscle power.

There are methods of making cultured butter that require far less of a workout, but I highly recommend making butter using this jar method at least once. If you don't, you will miss out on feeling the moment when the fat and whey break, or separate. Within one shake they break apart but exactly when it will happen is unknown. The suspense of the separation is reason enough to use this jar method. Did you ever imagine that butter churning could be so thrilling?

900 grams (32 ounces) heavy whipping cream

15 grams (2 tablespoons) mesophilic yogurt

1. Add heavy whipping cream and yogurt to a quart-size jar. Close lid of jar and shake gently to combine.

2. Leave to ferment at room temperature for 12–24 hours.

3. Once thick, place cultured cream in refrigerator until cold.

4. Separate cultured cream into 2 quart-size jars, close lids, and begin to shake one of them vigorously up and down.

5. Continue to shake. After a few minutes, the cream may turn nearly solid, a kind of quasi-whipped cream, but continue to shake it and the mass will eventually begin to move again.

6. Alternate shaking patterns if you are sore or exhausted. Hand off the duties to an unsuspecting person or take a short break if you really can't handle it.

7. Yes, continue to shake for what seems like forever. Shake, shake, and shake some more. Each jar will take anywhere from 5–20 minutes of shaking depending on how aggressive a shaker you are.

8. Suddenly you will experience a break between the milk fat and liquid. The butter has been released. Remove lid and pour off the liquid into a separate container. This liquid is real buttermilk. Drink it or use it in baking.

9. Place the nearly formed butter in a bowl of ice water and massage out any remaining buttermilk.

10. Remove from water and squeeze one last time to release liquid. Any remaining liquid will shorten the shelf life of the butter.

11. Shape butter into desired form, wrap or place in container, and refrigerate until ready to use.

12. Congratulate yourself for a laborious job well done. Next time you can use a food processor, but the consistency and texture may vary.

SMEN

This fermented butter is common in North Africa and the Middle East. The longer it ages, the more of an aged cheese aroma it develops. Try flavoring couscous with smen or use it in cooking anywhere you might use butter or oil.

500 grams (1 pound) butter

15 grams (1 tablespoon) salt

1. Melt the butter in a pot over low heat. Once melted, slowly bring to a boil and then simmer for 20–30 minutes until the milk solids have fully separated. This liquid is clarified butter.

2. Strain the clarified butter through fine cheesecloth. No milk solids should be in the clarified and strained butter. If necessary, strain more than once until only a clear liquid remains.

3. Combine salt and clarified butter in a quart-size jar. Stir to combine and then close lid.

4. Leave to ferment, away from direct sunlight and in a cool place, for 1–4 months. When ready to use refrigerate or store in a cool place.

SEASONED SMEN

Thyme or oregano is often added to the clarified butter before fermentation. Try it yourself by adding 12 grams (4 tablespoons) of dried oregano or thyme to the simmering butter. Remove by straining with the milk solids.

YIELD: 1 PINT

○ **PREP:** 5 minutes

▯ **FERMENTATION:** 12–24 hours

CULTURED WHIPPED CREAM

Looking for something a little classier than a tub of whipped cream from the grocery store? Then whip up this cultured cream for a sophisticated treat. And if you're lactose intolerant, then the predigestion of lactose, by way of fermentation, might make this a dessert topping that even you can enjoy.

If you don't have a whipped cream maker, you can still make this cultured whipped cream in a bowl with a whisk.

450 grams (16 ounces) heavy whipping cream

15 grams (1 tablespoon) mesophilic yogurt

15 grams (1 tablespoon) powdered sugar

4 grams (1 teaspoon) vanilla extract

1. Add heavy whipping cream and yogurt to a jar. Close lid of jar and shake gently to combine.

2. Leave to ferment at room temperature for 12–24 hours.

3. Once thick, place cultured cream in refrigerator and place metal whipped cream maker in freezer until both are chilled, about 30 minutes to 1 hour.

4. Pour or spoon the cultured cream into the whipped cream maker.

5. Add powdered sugar and vanilla extract into whipped cream maker.

6. Close the lid of the whipped cream maker, charge with nitrous oxide, shake, and serve.

7. Store unused whipped cream in refrigerator for up to 2 weeks.

Isn't This Crème Fraîche?

In the strictest sense, we are not using a proper crème fraîche starter culture (or raw milk) so this isn't a true crème fraîche. Many crème fraîche recipes also call for rennet and straining. But, yes, you could call this a whipped crème fraîche as long as you don't add sweetener or vanilla.

Cheese

Say "cheese" and remember to smile when attempting to make your first mozzarella. Cheeses aren't really that difficult to make, but they do generally require a little more awareness than most other ferments in this book.

The first cheese I ever made was feta. It's an easy cheese to make and incorporates many of the principles of more advanced cheeses. So if you catch the cheese-fermenting bug, you will have a good foundation to build upon.

Mozzarella is easy to comprehend, but a few variables make it a little more difficult for a beginner. Mozzarella is a stretched curd cheese requiring an exact pH level and temperature in order to stretch like melted plastic (this may not be the most appetizing description, but that's what it looks like). The stretch is what makes the added effort worth it. It is so much fun to play with and shape.

Ricotta made from whey is the easiest of them all, but it isn't the first recipe in this section because you will first need to collect whey from feta or mozzarella cheese making. The yield of cheese from whey is variable, so don't get your hopes up for making a lot of ricotta unless you find yourself swimming in whey.

It is important to use either pasteurized or raw milk in your cheese-making adventures. Do not attempt to make cheese from ultra-pasteurized, or UHT, milk. This extra high-heat pasteurization process makes milk shelf stable for longer, but it also makes it very difficult to form a good curd for cheese making.

It is also worth noting the importance of being extra clean when making cheese. Send all of your equipment through the dishwasher or submerge it in boiling water for at least 5 minutes before use.

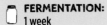

PREP: 3 hours

FERMENTATION:
1 week

FETA

This is the first cheese that I ever made and one that I recommend often to anyone who hasn't made cheese before. It's an easy cheese to make, and even if your execution isn't perfect on a few of the steps, more than likely only the texture will be affected and you will still end up with a deliciously edible end product.

1 gram (½ teaspoon) lipase powder

60 grams (¼ cup) + 60 grams (¼ cup) + 60 grams (¼ cup) water

9400 grams (2 gallons) whole milk, not ultra-pasteurized

1.5 grams (¼ teaspoon) Aroma B or other mesophilic feta starter culture

2 grams (½ teaspoon) calcium chloride

2 grams (½ teaspoon) liquid animal rennet

30 grams (2 tablespoons) kosher or flake salt

1. Dissolve lipase powder in 60 grams (¼ cup) of water.

2. In a large stockpot, combine milk and lipase powder solution.

3. Heat milk to 88°F (31°C) on medium-low heat. Remove from heat.

4. Add starter culture and allow to rehydrate for 2 minutes before stirring well to incorporate. Allow to ferment for 1 hour.

5. Dissolve calcium chloride in 60 grams (¼ cup) of water. Add to milk and stir gently to incorporate.

6. Dilute rennet in 60 grams (¼ cup) of water. Add to milk and stir with an up-and-down motion to thoroughly combine and distribute rennet.

7. Confirm temperature of milk is holding at 88°F (31°C) and return to heat if necessary. Do not overheat.

8. Leave milk to thicken and coagulate into curd for 1 hour until the whey begins to separate from the curd. To test this, use a clean knife and make a small incision into the curd. There should be a "clean break" and whey should begin to puddle at the point of incision.

(continued on following page)

9. Once there is a clean break, cut the curd into ½" cubes using a cake icing spatula or knife. First cut lines in one direction, rotate pot 90°, and the cut in the other direction to make cubes. In order to cut through the lower layers, use a diagonal cut by holding the spatula at an angle while making sweeping motions through the curd.

10. Allow curds to rest for 15 minutes and then gently stir for 15 minutes. Leave the curds to sink under the whey for another 5 minutes.

11. Line a large bowl with butter muslin or fine-mesh cheesecloth. Pour curds and whey into the bowl. Tie all 4 corners of the cheesecloth together and then lift from the bowl and allow the whey to strain.

12. Hang cheesecloth with a bowl underneath to catch intermittent drips of whey. Leave to drain and ferment for 6 hours at room temperature.

13. The curds should have formed a firm mass and taste mildly tart. Transfer the cheese to a cutting board and cut into 1" cubes.

14. Place the cubes of feta into a shallow plastic or glass container with fitting lid. Add salt to container, seal lid, and shake the contents gently until the surface of all feta cubes are salted.

15. Refrigerate for 1 week to allow the feta cubes to absorb the salt. Remove any whey that may collect inside the container daily. Consume within 2 weeks.

RELEASE THOSE FATTY ACIDS

Lipase is an enzyme present in raw milk that releases fatty acids from fat globules. It can optionally be added in powder form to create the traditional aroma and sharp taste often associated with feta and many other cheeses.

🕐 **PREP:** 4 hours

🫙 **FERMENTATION:**
1 day

MOZZARELLA

This isn't the easiest cheese to make, but it sure is fun to stretch when it all comes together. You can easily find recipes for "quick" mozzarellas that use an acid to bring the curd to the proper pH level for stretching, but those mozzarellas are not fermented. The following method will produce a fermented and more traditional mozzarella, although there is nothing quick about it.

Why go to the trouble of making homemade mozzarella? Freshness, taste, experience, and taste. Yes, the taste is worth mentioning twice. Book an entire day for your first mozzarella experience. You will be dealing with microbes, chemistry, and timing; they all have to line up for this one to work.

9400 grams (2 gallons) whole milk, not ultra-pasteurized

1.5 grams (¼ teaspoon) Thermo B or other mozzarella thermophilic starter culture (see Appendix)

2 grams (½ teaspoon) calcium chloride

60 grams (¼ cup) + 60 grams (¼ cup) water

2 grams (½ teaspoon) liquid animal rennet

15 grams (1 tablespoon) + 15 grams (1 tablespoon) salt

1900 grams (8 cups) ice cold water

1. Heat milk to 90°F (32°C) in a large stockpot on medium-low heat. Remove from heat.

2. Add starter culture and allow to rehydrate for 2 minutes before stirring well to incorporate. Allow to ferment for 45 minutes.

3. Dissolve calcium chloride in 60 grams (¼ cup) of water. Add to milk and stir gently to incorporate.

4. Dilute rennet in 60 grams (¼ cup) of water. Add to milk and stir with an up-and-down motion to thoroughly combine and distribute rennet.

5. Confirm temperature of milk is holding at 90°F (32°C) and return to heat if necessary. Do not overheat.

6. Leave milk to thicken and coagulate into curd for 45–60 minutes until the whey begins to separate from the curd. To test this, use a clean knife and make a small incision into the curd. There should be a "clean break" and whey should begin to puddle at the point of incision.

(continued on following page)

7. Once there is a clean break, cut the curd into ½" cubes using a cake icing spatula or knife. First cut lines in one direction, rotate pot 90°, and then cut in the other direction to make cubes. In order to cut through the lower layers, use a diagonal cut by holding the spatula at an angle while making sweeping motions through the curd.

8. Leave to sit for 15–30 minutes. Curd should begin to sink below the whey.

9. Slowly heat the curds and whey to 100°F (38°C) over a period of 20–30 minutes, stirring frequently. Remove from heat and allow curds to rest for 5 minutes.

10. Strain the whey from the curds using a colander or cheesecloth and reserve whey for later use.

11. Hold the curds at 105°F–110°F (40°C–43°C). This can be accomplished by filling a sink with 115°F (46°C) water and setting the pot of curds into the sink. Or use an incubator (see Chapter 1) for more accurate temperature control. Turn curd mass every 30 minutes for the first 2 hours.

12. If using a pH meter (optional), measure the pH every 30 minutes after the first 2 hours. Once the pH is close to 5, use the following step to stretch-test the curd. A stretch test is not required until the pH nears 5 and does not need to be performed every 30 minutes as is the case without a pH meter. This could be anywhere from 2–12 hours after straining the curd.

13. Perform a stretch test every 30 minutes after the first 2 hours. Wear heat-resistant or rubber dishwashing gloves and place a small chunk (about 1" square) of the curd into 170°F–180°F (77°C–82°C) water. After 30 seconds remove the curd from the water and fold it over itself a few times. Return to water and repeat 1–2 more times. Then attempt to stretch the curd. If it smoothly stretches at least 24", then your cheese is ready to stretch. If not, keep checking.

14. If the curd will not stretch smoothly within a few hours, continue to ferment and check every 2–3 hours from then on. Alternatively, refrigerate overnight and reheat the next morning and continue to perform stretch tests.

15. When a sample passes the stretch test, heat 1900 grams (8 cups) of previously reserved whey or water to 190°F (88°C). Add 15 grams salt to whey. Tear or cut remaining curd into 1" thick cubes.

16. Combine the remaining salt with ice water in a large bowl. Set aside.

17. Place the cut curd into a large bowl. Wearing heat-resistant gloves, pour the hot whey into the bowl and submerge the curd. Leave to sit for 1 minute.

18. Either with gloves or large wooden spoons, begin to press the curd together. Fold over as if kneading dough. The curd will begin to transform into a stretchy and shiny mass. Remove from water and stretch a few times. Return to water and repeat.

19. Return to hot water again. Remove and fold the mozzarella into a tight ball. If necessary, add to water again to smooth surface and bind seams.

20. As soon as ball is formed, submerge mozzarella into the prepared bowl of salt and ice water for 1 hour.

21. Wrap mozzarella tightly in plastic and refrigerate. Note that mozzarella will melt on pizza better if refrigerated for at least 2 days.

No Wasted Mistakes

If your mozzarella fails to stretch, it most likely won't melt either. It may not work for pizza but the cheese itself is still edible. Crumble it onto a salad or use its non-melting quality to your advantage by frying it up in a pan with oil or butter.

RICOTTA

This is a whey cheese made by extracting the last bit of milk protein from whey. It may not look like any more solids are in your whey, but heat it up and it may surprise you.

Whey from cheese or yogurt

1. Heat whey on medium heat until remaining milk solids separate. This will usually happen around 180°F–190°F (82°C–88°C) but a thermometer is not necessary.

2. Skim off the milk solids with a slotted spoon and place in a sieve or colander lined with butter muslin or fine cheesecloth. Allow remaining whey to drip for a few minutes up to 2 hours. The longer it strains, the thicker the resulting ricotta.

3. This cheese does not store well. Use within 2–4 days.

Chapter 4

GRAIN FERMENTATION

Grains are fermented for food and, in the case of beer, for alcohol. This chapter will focus on food-based ferments, specifically on how to make a sourdough starter for bread, how to soak grains to make them sour and more bio-available, and how to ferment gluten-free pancakes. We'll finish off with our first look at mold as fermentation agent.

🕐 **PREP:** 20 minutes

🫙 **FERMENTATION:** 1–10 days

SOUR MILLET

Leave cracked millet to soak in water for a few days and it transforms into a sour grain ready to be cooked into a thick porridge. The longer it sours, the more garlic and onion the porridge can stand up against. Millet can be cracked using a pestle and mortar, blender, food processor, or spice grinder. It is only necessary to break the grains in half, but any level of cracking, except as fine as flour, will work.

200 grams (1 cup) millet, cracked

Water for soaking

250 grams (1 cup) water

5 cloves garlic, minced

3 green onions, diced

Crushed red pepper (optional)

Salt to taste

Black pepper to taste, freshly

1. Soak millet in water for 1–10 days. If water shows signs of turning grey, discard or use same day. Stir daily if fermenting for more than 4 days to avoid grey water.

2. Drain water and place millet in a pot with fresh water. Cook on medium-high heat, stirring constantly for 5–15 minutes until millet thickens into the consistency of porridge.

3. Remove from heat and add garlic, green onions, red pepper, salt, and black pepper.

4. Allow flavors to sit and absorb for 5 minutes and then serve.

SOAKING YOUR OATMEAL

Oatmeal also benefits from being soaked and is easy to start the night prior to breakfast. Soak in water or yogurt for at least 6 hours and up to 2 days. Then cook in soaking liquid and enjoy.

SOURDOUGH STARTER

Making sourdough starter at home is about as easy as it gets (especially when compared to the much greater challenge of making superb leavened bread with the starter). Unless your kitchen is sterile (not likely), plenty of wild yeast exists in your home, and you can capture it in a jar. A mixture of flour and water left at room temperature will become a food source for these wild yeasts.

If by chance your flour and water begin to mold, toss them out and start over. Over the years of initiating new sourdough starters I have only had this happen a few times. If you successfully feed your sourdough starter on schedule, it can live indefinitely and may outlive you.

FOR DAY ONE:

90 grams (½ cup) whole wheat, rye, or all-purpose flour

90 grams (⅓ cup) water

FOR DAY TWO:

90 grams (½ cup) whole wheat, rye, or all-purpose flour

90 grams (⅓ cup) water

FOR DAY THREE AND BEYOND:

60 grams (⅓ cup) whole wheat, rye, or all-purpose flour

60 grams (¼ cup) water

1. Day One: Combine flour and water in a quart-size jar and stir. Cover with cheesecloth or coffee filter secured with a rubber band. Leave to ferment in a warm location for 24 hours.

2. Day Two: Bubbles may or may not be present. Discard half of the starter and add new flour and water. Stir and cover for 24 hours.

3. Day Three: Bubbles and yeast activity should now be visible. Discard half of the starter and add new flour and water. Stir and cover for 24 hours.

4. Day Four: Repeat Day Three.

5. Day Five: Repeat Day Four, each day, until sourdough starter shows signs of active bubbling soon after feeding and smells mildly sour and yeast-like. This could be on Day Five or Ten depending on your environment.

6. Once active, sourdough starter is ready for use in baking. Unused starter may be stored at room temperature, but it will require feeding at least every other day. Sourdough starter may also be stored in the refrigerator but must be removed and fed once a week at room temperature for at least 12 hours before returning to the refrigerator.

7. Sourdough starter can last indefinitely if properly cared for. Sourdough yeast and bacteria are hardy, so even if you miss a feeding or two, it is usually possible to bring the starter back to health. Enjoy your new pet.

Sourdough Saver

If you wish not to discard excess starter, then store a separate jar in the refrigerator for any leftover starter until you have enough to use for one of the sourdough recipes in Chapter 8. When ready to use, feed and bring to room temperature like you would a regular starter.

DOSA-INSPIRED PANCAKES

These pancakes are thicker than a traditional dosa but the fermentation process is similar. The texture is more like a traditional pancake, albeit less fluffy, and they are easier to pour than the paper-thin original. These taste great with any savory topping such as a chutney, curry, peanut butter, or with the following kimchi-infused honey.

FOR PANCAKES:

370 grams (2 cups) white rice

185 grams (1 cup) brown, red, or green lentils

8 grams (½ tablespoon) salt

1000 grams (4 cups) water

Coconut, sesame, or other cooking oil

FOR HONEY (OPTIONAL):

165 grams (½ cup) honey

80 grams (¼ cup) Red Kimchi (see Chapter 2)

1. Place rice and lentils in a bowl and fill with water. Cover with plate or towel and let soak for 24 hours at room temperature.

2. On the following day pour off half of the soak water and then puree the rice, lentils, salt, and remaining water in a food processor, blender, or by using a pestle and mortar. The batter should now resemble a semi-thick pancake batter. Add more water if needed. Cover and let sit for 1–2 more days at room temperature.

3. Once the rice and lentil batter has visibly risen, it is ready to cook. Do not let the batter sit for too long after rising or the final pancake will be flat and sour due to overfermentation.

4. If preparing the kimchi-infused honey, heat honey and kimchi in a double boiler, or bowl on top of a saucepan, on medium low for 5–10 minutes. Strain kimchi solids and reserve honey.

5. Warm a pan on medium heat. Brush with a thin coat of coconut or sesame oil before each new pancake. Pour roughly 1 cup of batter per pancake and allow the pancakes to settle on their own. Cook for 2–3 minutes per side, flipping once.

6. Serve warm or at room temperature with cultured butter and kimchi-infused honey.

Thick Like Idli

This batter is similar in thickness to idli, another traditional Indian ferment. The main difference is that idli batter is steamed instead of cooked in a pan.

RICE KOJI

The smell of sweet and fruity koji will grow on you. Either after the first few inhalations or once you've worked with koji multiple times, the allure will take hold.

If you want to make Amazake (see Chapter 6) or Sweet White Miso (see Chapter 5) then you will need to make or purchase koji. Rice or barley koji are grains inoculated with the mold *Aspergillus oryzae*. Making koji is simple, but depending on your home setup, it may take a few attempts before you perfect your technique. However, it is a rewarding endeavor and well worth the attempt (and a lot cheaper than buying it in the store).

The amount of koji starter will be dependent on where you source your starter. There are different forms of starter, and some are more potent than others. Calculate the amount based on the recommendation of your starter supplier.

900 grams (4½ cups) white rice

2 grams (1½ teaspoons) koji starter

1. Rinse rice in cold water until water is no longer cloudy. Soak rice in water for at least 12 hours.

2. Drain water from rice. Option A: If using a bamboo steamer, line the steamer with butter muslin or fine-mesh cheesecloth and steam rice for 50 minutes. Depending on the size of steamer, this may require multiple batches. Option B: If using a pressure cooker, place the rice in a stainless steel colander small enough to fit inside the pressure cooker. Add 375 grams (1½ cups) water, or the minimum amount of water required for your pressure cooker, whichever is greater. Seal and heat to 15 PSI, hold for 30 seconds, and then remove from heat and allow to depressurize for about 10 minutes.

(continued on following page)

3. Remove rice from steamer or pressure cooker and place in a glass cake pan. Once cool enough to touch, use very clean hands to stir and work out any clumps that have formed. Continue to stir until rice has cooled to 110°F (43°C).

4. Add koji starter to rice and mix thoroughly for 5 minutes.

5. Cover with a clean and damp cloth. Incubate at 86°F (30°C) for 6 hours. If possible, control your incubator's temperature based on the internal temperature of the rice by inserting the probe into the middle of the rice bed. If this is not possible, check the internal temperature with a thermometer every few hours to make certain it remains near 86°F (30°C).

6. After the first 6 hours, stir rice and break up any clumps that have formed. Cover and return to incubator for another 6 hours.

7. Stir rice again and if rice feels drier than before, re-dampen cloth, cover, and return to incubator for another 12 hours.

8. Rice should smell faintly sweet. Stir rice one more time and then create 2–3 trenches or furrows in the rice bed. Only make the trenches halfway deep and do not expose the bottom of the cake pan. The goal is to create as much surface area as possible and decrease likelihood of overheating as the koji mold grows. Cover and incubate for 12 more hours, ensuring that the temperature remains near 86°F (30°C).

9. Check rice and dampness of cloth. If necessary, lightly re-dampen the cloth. Rice should smell sweet and fragrant and have signs of a white fuzzy mold beginning to form. Cover and ferment for another 8–12 hours.

10. Once a white mold has stretched across the rice bed, remove from incubator, break up the rice clumps, and bring to room temperature. Use rice koji immediately, refrigerate or freeze in a sealed container, or slowly dry for 1–2 days for longer-term storage. Refrigerated koji will keep for 2–4 weeks, dry koji for 3–6 months, and frozen koji for up to 1 year.

UNDER PRESSURE

If you want to make a lot of koji, I recommend using a 20-quart or larger pressure cooker. I like to make 4 pounds at a time, and steaming 1 batch of rice in a pressure cooker saves a lot of time compared to multiple batches in a steamer.

CHAPTER 5

LEGUME FERMENTATION

The legume ferments in this chapter come from Southeast Asia, China, and Japan. The history of these ferments is long, each having gone through much change before becoming what we know today.

It is only relatively recently that these ferments have become popular in Western countries. This popularity is giving rise to experimentation and cross-cultural ferment manipulation. Using Eastern techniques along with Western ingredients opens whole new realms of possibility in taste and consumption.

Start with these basic, but not necessarily traditional, recipes and then start to experiment with other legumes and grains using the same techniques. You could be the next person to discover some new and exciting flavor combination that wows the world.

YIELD: 1 QUART

🕐 **PREP:** 30 minutes

🫙 **FERMENTATION:** 4–6 weeks

SWEET WHITE MISO

This is the simplest and quickest miso ferment to make at home. Many styles of miso take months or years to ferment, but this one can be finished in 1–2 months. This miso uses more koji and less salt than longer ferments. As the name implies, it is also sweeter than other miso recipes, having a much more prominent koji flavor. Substitute another legume of your choosing for soybeans if desired.

Note that a commercially available miso may be used for the last ingredient as long as it is unpasteurized. It does not need be a sweet white miso; any style of miso will work.

200 grams (1 cup) soybeans, dried

30 grams (2 tablespoons) salt

230 grams (1 cup) cooking water from soybeans

400 grams (3 cups) Rice Koji (see Chapter 4)

10 grams (1 tablespoon) unpasteurized miso

Salt for surface

1. Soak soybeans for 12 hours.

2. Drain soybeans, add to a large pot, and cover with water. Bring to a boil and simmer for 4–6 hours, or until soybeans can easily be crushed between fingers. Alternatively, use a pressure cooker and cook at 15 PSI for 30 minutes and allow to depressurize naturally. Use caution when pressure-cooking soybeans because the hulls can clog vents. This is easier to avoid with a large pressure cooker.

3. Drain soybeans but reserve 1 cup of the cooking water.

4. Combine cooked soybeans, salt, and cooking water in a bowl. Mash together with a potato masher or the back of a large spoon until blended. Leave some semi-whole beans and do not mash completely.

5. Allow to cool to at least 140°F (60°C) and then add rice koji and unpasteurized miso. Combine thoroughly.

6. Pack the mixture into a half-gallon-size flip-top glass jar. Make certain to expel any air pockets in the soybean mixture while packing. Press firmly to flatten the surface of the mixture.

7. Wipe down the inner walls and mouth of the jar. Coat the top surface with a light dusting of salt.

8. Seal jar and leave to ferment, away from direct sunlight, for 4–6 weeks. If using a screw-top jar, check regularly for buildup of pressure and release when necessary by quickly opening and closing the lid. If using a flip-top jar, no release of pressure should be necessary.

9. When finished fermenting, pour off liquid and use as flavoring agent (this is tamari) and transfer miso to a smaller jar for storage in a refrigerator.

CHICKPEA AND WILD RICE TEMPEH

If this is your first time trying homemade tempeh, then you are in for a treat. Unless you live in a market with access to high-quality fresh tempeh, nothing will compare to the homemade stuff.

If you do not have a grain mill for cracking the dry beans, you can skip that step and lightly mash the chickpeas, once cooked, in order to make it easier for the tempeh mold to penetrate the bean surface. If you do not have a pressure cooker, you will need to boil chickpeas for 45 minutes and then drain and thoroughly dry the chickpeas with towels or a hair dryer.

This same recipe can be used to make soybean tempeh. Just substitute soybeans for the chickpeas and short grain white rice for the wild rice.

900 grams (4½ cups) chickpeas

180 grams (1 cup) wild rice

120 grams (½ cup) vinegar

75 grams (⅓ cup) water

1 gram (½ teaspoon) tempeh starter

1. Using a hand-crank corn or grain mill on the widest setting, crack the chickpeas in half.

2. Soak chickpeas in water for 8–12 hours. Remove any hulls that float to the surface of the water.

3. Drain chickpeas and add to a pressure cooker along with the wild rice, vinegar, and water. Stir to combine.

4. Seal and bring pressure cooker to 15 PSI and cook for 7 minutes. Remove from heat and submerge in cold water to depressurize.

5. Drain off remaining liquid, if any, and transfer chickpeas to a large bowl and stir to cool to 95°F (35°C).

6. Stir in tempeh starter. Continue to stir for at least 1 minute to ensure full coverage.

7. Spread evenly into an extra-large cake pan or full-size stainless steel restaurant steam table pan (can be ordered online or found at a local restaurant supply store) and gently compress.

8. Incubate at 86°F (30°C) and 85–95% humidity for 24–36 hours. This is most easily accomplished using an aquarium heater in a large plastic tub filled with water (see Understanding Temperature in Chapter 1). If using the aquarium heater method, set the pan on the water. The pan will float on the surface. Gently rest the lid on the tub, and cover with thick blankets.

9. Once a thick mat of white mold has covered the chickpeas, the tempeh is ready to harvest. If black spots have begun to form, this is a sign that the mold has begun to sporulate. This is generally considered harmless. Remove tempeh from incubator and cut tempeh into single-use portions.

10. Store in plastic and refrigerate for up to 1 week or freeze for months.

- ⏱ **PREP:** 30 minutes
- 🫙 **FERMENTATION:** 12–24 hours

CANNED CHICKPEA NATTō

This slimy treat is delicious. Yes, slimy is a positive attribute in this case. I love it, but you may need to acquire a taste for nattō's unique flavor and texture.

If you're making nattō at home, it is important to maintain a clean working environment and use clean utensils. If you encounter issues making nattō, then you may need to go full-blown sterilized. In an attempt to make the nattō process as simple as possible, I'm using canned organic chickpeas in this recipe instead of soybeans. They don't require the long cooking time of soybeans and they don't come out quite as slimy.

500 grams (2 15-ounce cans) organic chickpeas

Enough boiling water to cover beans

0.05 grams (a dash) nattō starter

8 grams (2 teaspoons) water

1. Sterilize a piece of muslin or cheesecloth in boiling water for 5 minutes. This cloth will be used to capture condensation in the sealed containers with nattō. You may also wish to boil all utensils, bowls, and containers used for nattō making at this time.

2. Drain and rinse beans. Place beans in a large bowl and submerge under boiling water for 1 minute.

3. Dissolve starter into water in a small bowl.

4. Drain beans and return to large bowl. Immediately pour starter and water over beans and stir until thoroughly combined.

5. Transfer beans to a flat glass container with lid. Beans should be layered no more than 1" high. Use multiple containers if necessary.

6. Cover the container with the sterilized muslin and then seal with lid. Incubate at 101°F (38°C) for 12–24 hours.

7. Once fermented, remove from incubation, and allow to cool to room temperature. Then remove lid and muslin. Quickly wash and dry lid and reseal on container. Refrigerate nattō for at least 6 hours before serving. If nattō is not slimy when stirred, discard and try again.

CHAPTER 6

BEVERAGE FERMENTATION

Let's get the big warning out of the way first: If you ferment beverages in sealed glass, there is a risk that bottles could explode from a buildup of carbonation when left to ferment at room temperature for longer than necessary. Before this happened to me, I had only heard that it was possible but had never found any eyewitness accounts of it.

I don't do this anymore. Not since a bottle exploded in my kitchen, sending small shards of glass a surprising distance. Worse yet, my wife and infant son had been in the kitchen minutes before the explosion. We found shards of glass throughout the house for more than a week. Had anyone been in the kitchen, the explosion could have caused serious injuries if not death.

If you're using glass to ferment beverages, do so behind the closed doors of a cabinet or in a box. This way, if the bottle explodes, it will remain contained. Ferment only in glass bottles made for carbonated beverages. Flip-top beer bottles work great, but not all flip-top bottles are created equal. It was a flip-top bottle that I used when the accident occurred, but it was one that was cheap and most likely not intended to contain pressure. Finally, monitor your ferments and move them to cooler temperatures or refrigeration once the carbonation stage is complete.

Fermented beverages are a lot of fun to produce. The alcoholic ferments throughout this chapter are spontaneous ferments using wild yeasts. This means the alcohol content will not be as high as from commercially available yeasts. The one exception is rice beer, which uses a starter culture commonly found at Asian grocery stores. If left to ferment long enough, this rice beer can acquire much higher alcohol levels than other beverages in this chapter.

KOMBUCHA

Kombucha is a sweet-and-sour beverage produced by fermentation from both bacteria and yeast in a sugar tea solution. This symbiotic colony of bacteria and yeast (SCOBY) forms a gelatinous film on the surface of the brewing liquid. This is very similar to the mother of vinegar found in the process of making vinegar.

This is one of those ferments that is way cheaper to make than purchase from the store once you find yourself a SCOBY from a friend, purchase one, or grow one from a bottle of store-bought brew.

3700 grams (1 gallon) water

25 grams (⅓ cup) loose-leaf green tea or 8 tea bags

225 grams (1 cup) sugar

1 kombucha SCOBY

1. Bring ¼ of the water to a boil. Remove water from heat and use to steep tea for recommended length of time. As a general guideline, steep green tea for 1–3 minutes and black tea for 2–5 minutes.

2. Remove tea leaves. Add sugar to brewed tea and stir until dissolved.

3. Pour tea into a gallon-size jar. Add remaining water to the jar. This should dilute and cool the sweet tea to approximately room or body temperature. If tea is still hot, wait for it to cool before moving on to next step.

4. Add kombucha SCOBY to the jar. The SCOBY may sink or float and does not affect the final brew.

5. Leave to ferment, away from direct sunlight, for 1–4 weeks until sufficiently sour.

6. When taste is to your liking, remove SCOBY and pour the newly fermented kombucha into 1 or more jars or bottles.

7. Optionally add flavorings such as herbs or fruit to the kombucha, seal lids, and leave to ferment for up to 2 more weeks. This second stage of fermentation adds carbonation.

8. Refrigerate or ice before serving.

Know Your Teas

If you want your kombucha SCOBY to thrive, use only tea made from the leaves of the *Camellia sinensis* shrub. This includes black, green, oolong, and white teas.

GROW YOUR OWN SCOBY

While it is becoming much easier to source a kombucha SCOBY from an online retailer or local workshop in many areas, you can just as easily pick up a bottle of kombucha at the grocery store and grow your own SCOBY. Small and local brands are most likely to work best.

1 (16-ounce) bottle kombucha

1. Pour entire bottle of store-bought kombucha into a large and shallow glass bowl. The more surface area, the better and faster the SCOBY will grow.

2. Cover bowl with fabric or cheesecloth. Secure fabric to bowl using a rubber band or string.

3. Leave to ferment, away from direct sunlight, for 1–3 weeks until a thick film forms and much of the liquid has diminished. This is best accomplished in warmer weather. Otherwise the process could take 2–3 times as long during a cold winter.

4. Use this new SCOBY to make future batches of kombucha.

PREP: 5 minutes

READY IN: 5 minutes

AYRAN YOGURT DRINK

Ayran is a Turkish yogurt beverage, and Tahn is the Armenian equivalent. Whatever you call it, this beverage is surprisingly refreshing on a hot summer day.

240 grams (1 cup) yogurt

240 grams (1 cup) water

Pinch of salt

1. Combine yogurt, water, and salt in a blender, bowl, jar, or pitcher. Blend, shake, or stir until combined. Try adding water slowly during the mixing process for a foamier version.

2. Pour into glasses and serve immediately or store in refrigerator for up to 1 hour for a colder beverage.

ALCOHOL CONTENT

Some of the sugar in kombucha is converted into ethanol during the fermentation process but the finished beverage's alcohol content is generally below 2%.

YIELD: 1 QUART

⏱ **PREP:** 5 minutes
🫙 **FERMENTATION:**
1–3 days

WATER KEFIR

Water kefir grains are used to inoculate fresh batches of sugar water. Within a few days you will have a fizzy beverage.

You can use an assortment of substrates with water kefir. Fruit juices and other sugary liquids are begging for you to ferment them. Just be sure to keep a pure culture of water kefir grains (they multiply quickly) fed solely on sugar water. This is an extra precaution so as not to lose your grains if they ever fail to thrive in a specific substrate.

As with many starter cultures, water kefir grains can be procured fresh or dehydrated. Either will work, although it will take extra time to rehydrate dried ones.

950 grams (4 cups) water

55 grams (4 tablespoons) sugar

50 grams (4 tablespoons) water kefir grains

1. Combine water and sugar in jar, seal with lid, and shake until sugar dissolves.

2. Remove lid and add water kefir grains to jar.

3. Cover with cloth, paper towel, or coffee filter.

4. Leave to ferment, away from direct sunlight, for 1–3 days. If left too long, the grains will begin to disintegrate.

5. Pour liquid through a fine-mesh strainer. Place strained water kefir grains in a clean jar and repeat previous steps.

6. Seal and refrigerate the fermented water kefir for a sweet but relatively flat beverage or, alternatively, leave the sealed bottle or jar at room temperature for 1 day to 2 weeks in order to create a carbonated beverage before refrigerating.

Too Sweet?

If the sugar water is too sweet for you after 3 days, then allow the liquid to ferment without grains until properly sour. This second stage of fermentation is also the perfect time to add flavorings to plain water kefir.

YIELD: 1 QUART

🕐 **PREP:** 10 minutes

🫙 **FERMENTATION:** 1–10 days

GINGER BEER PLANT

You will first need to source a ginger beer plant if you want to make this old world small beer. Ginger beer plant (a.k.a. GBP or beeswine) is very similar in appearance to water kefir grain except it contains a different colony of bacteria and yeast and the grains tend to be smaller. If you can't easily obtain a GBP culture, you can flavor water kefir with ginger for a similar beverage.

800 grams (3½ cups) water

100 grams (½ cup) brown sugar

25 grams (about 2") ginger root, peeled and bruised

1 gram (¼ teaspoon) citric acid or lemon slice

0.5 grams (¼ teaspoon) tartaric acid or cream of tartar

20–50 grams (2–4 tablespoons) Ginger Beer Plant (see Appendix)

1 star anise (optional)

10 juniper berries, bruised (optional)

1. Place water, sugar, ginger, citric acid, and tartaric acid into a quart-size jar. Close lid and shake vigorously until most of the sugar has dissolved.

2. Open jar and add ginger beer plant. Cover jar with cloth or coffee filter and secure with rubber band or string. Leave to ferment in a warm place for 1–3 days. If not actively bubbling, move to a warmer location and leave to ferment until it does.

3. Strain the ginger beer through a fine-mesh sieve. Remove ginger and discard. Use the ginger beer plant immediately for a subsequent batch of ginger beer repeating the first 2 steps.

4. Optionally, add the star anise and juniper berries (or any flavoring you can imagine) to the filtered ginger beer. Continue to ferment the ginger beer in a closed container for 3 or more days until sweetness is to your liking.

DEHYDRATED PLANTS

You can order ginger beer plant online in either fresh or dehydrated form. If using fresh GBP, you can follow this recipe immediately. Otherwise, first follow the instructions provided with your dried culture.

AMAZAKE

This is a sweet rice beverage made using rice koji. First you will make an amazake mash, which will be heated with equal parts water for a warm amazake beverage. Beyond making a beverage, the mash can be eaten as a sweet porridge or used as a sugar substitute in baking.

FOR AMAZAKE MASH:

400 grams (2 cups) dry brown rice

1200 grams (5 cups) water

260 grams (2 cups) Rice Koji (see Chapter 4)

FOR WARM AMAZAKE:

240 grams (1 cup) amazake mash

240 grams (1 cup) water

1. Combine brown rice and water in a pot and bring to a gentle boil. Once boiling, cover and cook on low for 50 minutes. Remove from heat and allow to sit covered for 10 minutes.

2. Remove cooked rice from pot and place in a glass cake pan. The rice will be slightly overcooked and mushy. Allow to cool to at least 150°F (65°C). Constant stirring can speed up cooling but is not necessary.

3. Combine koji with rice and stir with spoon or clean hands until evenly dispersed.

4. Cover with pan lid or plastic wrap and place in a warm place or incubate at 120°F (50°C) for 6–12 hours. Open and stir thoroughly every 1–2 hours. Taste at each stirring interval to better understand the transformation and to sample for doneness.

5. The amazake mash will smell and taste sweet when done. If mash begins to taste sour, then the enzymatic process has progressed too far. It is still usable if sour but stop incubation sooner next time.

6. Place amazake mash into a pot and bring to a boil and then simmer for 3–5 minutes. The heat halts the enzymatic process and kills any yeast that would otherwise continue to convert available sugars into alcohol.

7. Puree the heated amazake mash in a blender or food processor for a smooth texture (optional).

8. For a warm amazake beverage, heat equal parts amazake mash and water in a pot until warm. Serve in mugs dusted with powdered or freshly grated ginger. Nutmeg works too.

If your bread ever goes stale, use it to make kvass, a refreshing and carbonated Russian beverage with a mild beer flavor. If you catch the kvass bug, you may soon be making or buying bread with the sole intention of letting it stale on purpose. Fresh bread can also be used.

YIELD: 2 GALLONS

🕐 **PREP:** 30 minutes

🫙 **FERMENTATION:** 1–3 weeks

450 grams (1 pound) stale or fresh bread, sliced

9 kilograms (2½ gallons or 10 quarts) water

Raisins

725 grams (4 cups) sugar

250 grams (1 cup) Sourdough Starter (see Chapter 4)

1. Toast bread in a toaster or directly on racks in an oven preheated to 400°F (205°C) until dark. The darker the bread is toasted, the darker and more flavorful the final beverage. Don't be afraid to burn it but be sure to have proper ventilation for smoke.

2. Bring water to a boil in a large stockpot. Remove from heat and add a handful of raisins and toasted bread slices. Cover and leave to soak for at least 8 hours.

3. Remove and discard bread. Add sugar and sourdough starter to the pot and stir. Cover and leave to ferment for 8 hours, stirring every couple of hours (or as often as possible).

4. The kvass should now be actively bubbling. Add any optional flavorings at this time. Leave to ferment for up to 1 week in the pot or strain and bottle immediately.

5. When ready to bottle, first remove floating raisins. Gently pour kvass into plastic or glass bottles, leaving most of the sediment behind. Note: If using glass, be cautious of over-fermentation and the potential of exploding bottles.

6. Add 2–3 raisins to each jar. Close lids, and leave to ferment in a cool place until the raisins float to the top. This is a sign of carbonation.

7. Refrigerate bottles until ready to serve.

OPTIONAL FLAVORS

Try adding mint, lemon, or hops for a flavored brew.

APPLE CIDER

The first time I tried hard apple cider fermentation, I simply purchased a gallon of pasteurized organic apple juice, removed the lid, and covered it with a cloth. In subsequent batches, I have either made juice from whole apples or purchased raw apple cider. The fermentation process begins much quicker when starting with a non-pasteurized juice, but either approach will be capable of capturing wild yeast.

YIELD: 1 GALLON

🕐 **PREP:** 5 minutes

🫙 **FERMENTATION:** 1–6 weeks

1 gallon organic apple juice

1. Remove lid from apple juice container and cover with a cloth, paper towel, or coffee filter. Secure with rubber band or string.

2. Alternatively, transfer apple juice to a container with more surface area in order to create a larger platform for aeration and wild yeasts.

3. Stir or swirl apple juice daily (especially important if using pasteurized juice) until bubbles begin to form rapidly. If surface mold forms (skim it off), this is a sign you are not stirring frequently enough.

4. Once actively bubbling, either leave in current container, or transfer juice to a gallon jug with airlock.

5. Leave to ferment, away from direct sunlight, for 1 week to 1 month for a mildly alcoholic cider.

BOOST YOUR JUICE

Not legal to buy raw apple juice where you live and don't have time to press your own apples? Then give your pasteurized apple juice a boost of fresh microorganisms by tossing in a few quartered organic apples at the beginning of the fermentation process.

MEAD

Mead, or honey wine, is simple to make and requires only 2 ingredients: honey and water. This mead is wild yet mild. The wild yeasts that ferment this beverage won't be capable of producing the same high levels of alcohol that a commercial yeast strain could. If you're looking to get drunk, this mead is probably too sweet for that. Instead, if you're interested in exploring the process of converting an antimicrobial product, such as honey, into a highly fermentable substrate simply by adding water, then get ready to party with some wild yeast.

Raw honey will be easier to work with considering some of the necessary yeasts may already be present, but I have also successfully cultured heated honey. The key is in aerating the brew regularly until it starts to actively bubble. Uncover the honey water and stir to create a whirlpool in a clockwise and counterclockwise direction. Do this at least twice a day or mold may form on the surface. If mold does appear, catch it soon enough and you can simply scrape it off. Mold is a sign that you are not stirring frequently enough. If you're short on time, then at least give the jar a swirl or two throughout the day. Mold doesn't thrive well on a moving surface. So remember to move, swirl, and stir.

450 grams (1 pound) honey, raw or heated

1600 grams (7 cups) water

1. Combine honey and water in a glass jar, stirring until honey dissolves.

2. Cover with cloth, paper towel, or coffee filter and leave to ferment, away from direct sunlight, for 1–4 weeks.

3. Make certain to stir multiple times each day in order to avoid mold.

4. Mead is ready to enjoy once bubbling subsides.

RICE BEER

Many people know sake, but that isn't the only rice beer in the world. Similar rice beer beverages are found throughout Asia. This one is very simple to make but depending on where you are located, it may be difficult to find Chinese yeast balls, often transliterated as "chu" or "qu." If you cannot find them at a local Asian market, you can purchase them online. Only 1 Chinese yeast ball is required for this recipe, but 2 will speed up the process.

YIELD: 1 QUART

🕐 **PREP:** 15 minutes

🫙 **FERMENTATION:**
1–3 weeks

420 grams (2 cups) brown rice

1200 grams (5 cups) water

1 or 2 Chinese yeast balls

1. Place rice and water in a pot and bring to a boil. Cover and cook on low for 50 minutes.

2. Cool rice to 100°F (38°C) or roughly body temperature.

3. Crush the Chinese yeast ball with a pestle and mortar, place in a plastic bag and crush with a blunt object, or use an electric spice grinder.

4. Mix the powdered yeast ball into the rice by hand. Ensure that the yeast powder has been thoroughly mixed.

5. Place rice mixture in a glass or plastic vessel with lid. Create a well in the center. Cover with lid and leave to sit in a warm location for 2 days.

6. After 2 days, the well should be filled with liquid. This is the beginning of the rice beer. It should smell sweet. Cover with cloth or paper towel and leave to sit in a warm place for 1–2 weeks. Note: If no liquid has formed, leave to ferment with lid on, checking daily for liquid. If liquid has not formed within 1 week, discard and try again.

7. After 1–2 weeks, the liquid should smell alcoholic and mildly sweet. Strain the liquid through a fine-mesh cheesecloth and discard the rice solids.

8. Seal the rice beer liquid in a bottle or jar. Leave at room temperature for another few days to build carbonation. Refrigerate and serve.

PART 2

USING YOUR FERMENTS

You made it this far. Either you've skipped ahead, or you now have a fully equipped refrigerator, pantry, basement, or root cellar full of ferments. This section will explore how to use and cook with ferments beyond using them as side dishes or snacks.

Every recipe in this section includes at least 1 ferment from Part I, and some contain many. Don't feel obligated to make every single one yourself. You can incorporate more fermented foods into your life whether you are making or buying them. This section will show you how.

CHAPTER 7

RICE AND PASTAS

Use the recipes in this section as a jumping-off point to creating your own dishes. Pasta and rice provide an excellent canvas for your fermented foods. You can lean on them heavily for flavor or cover them up with stronger tastes. There is plenty of room for ferment experimentation.

When I was younger, I lived off of rice and pastas. I'll admit that they were often boring and plain dishes (ramen noodles all day long), so eventually I stopped being lazy and began spending more than a few minutes on breakfasts, lunches, or dinners.

Pasta still holds a special place in my heart, but instead of purchasing dried pasta, I now like to make it myself. Don't be intimidated by the process of making your own pastas from scratch. Homemade pasta is really tough to mess up. As with so many things in the kitchen, it may take a few times before you make it just the way you like it, but these kitchen experiments are supposed to be about the journey, right?

🕐 **PREP:** 30 minutes
⏲ **READY IN:** 20 minutes

NATTŌ FRIED RICE

Unsure about the slimy consistency of nattō or have friends and family that can't stand it? Then acquire a taste for it slowly by hiding it in this fried rice. The nattō imparts a mild nutty flavor to the dish but the ropy, or slimy, texture disappears. Yet this isn't just a cover-up kind of meal; it is a memorable fried rice dish in its own right.

40 grams (3 tablespoons) bacon grease or cooking oil

1 large carrot, thinly sliced

1 large parsnip, thinly sliced

A few purple cabbage leaves, torn

640 grams (4 cups) cooked rice, day old

50 grams (3 tablespoons) soy sauce

1 large egg

350 grams (2 cups) Canned Chickpea Nattō (see Chapter 5)

5 grams (½ tablespoon) red pepper, crushed or powder

Sesame seeds

1. Heat wok or pan on high heat. When preheated, add bacon grease and heat until melted.

2. Add carrots and parsnips and cook for 2 minutes, stirring frequently.

3. Add cabbage leaves and cook for 2 minutes, stirring frequently.

4. Break up any clumps in rice and add to wok. Add soy sauce and stir until well combined.

5. Make a well in center and add egg. Scramble egg until done.

6. Remove from heat and stir in nattō and red pepper. Plate, garnish with sesame seeds, and serve.

ADDITIONAL FERMENTED FLAVOR

Fried rice is an excellent dumping ground for any leftover fermented vegetables. If you decide to add ferments to this dish, use less soy sauce to account for the added salt from the vegetables.

KIMCHI AND RICE

It doesn't take much to turn kimchi into a delicious meal. Some bacon and a couple of eggs make this a filling repast. This is one of those recipes where all of the ingredients play nicely together no matter the proportions. So if you love bacon then pile it on. If you only have a small portion of kimchi left at the bottom of a jar then use what you have and it will still taste great.

Lard, bacon grease, or cooking oil

2 large eggs

Bacon, diced

1 cup rice

Kimchi (see Chapter 2)

Sesame seeds

1. Heat a wok or pan on medium-high heat. Add lard. Fry 1 of the 2 eggs in the wok. Once fried to your liking, remove egg from wok and save to the side.

2. Add bacon to wok and cook until crispy, about 5–10 minutes, stirring occasionally.

3. Add second egg to wok and scramble with bacon.

4. Add rice and kimchi to wok and stir quickly to incorporate with bacon and scrambled egg until warm.

5. Transfer to a plate or bowl, top with fried egg, and garnish with sesame seeds. Serve immediately.

YOGURT PASTA DOUGH

Fresh pasta tastes amazing when done right. Some might say this recipe is a little wrong with the addition of yogurt, but I say it makes it doubly right. The yogurt adds a mild tart flavor and a slight creaminess that doesn't fall apart when cooked. I highly recommend a pasta maker for this recipe because you will want to make fresh pasta all of the time. It is possible to make this by hand rolling the dough but the yield may be smaller since you probably won't be able to roll it quite as thin as a pasta maker.

112 grams (1 cup) all-purpose flour

25 grams (1½ tablespoons) yogurt or Kefir (see Chapter 3)

1 large egg

1. Knead all ingredients together in a bowl until combined.

2. Let mixture rest for at least 30 minutes and up to 3 hours.

3. Run through pasta machine and cut into desired shape or hand roll and cut.

4. When ready to serve, boil in salted water for 1–2 minutes and then strain. Do not overcook.

PRECISE MEASUREMENTS

Instead of this recipe's measurements, I recommend weighing your egg first. Crack the egg into your bowl, weigh it, and then multiply the weight by 0.5 for your precise amount of yogurt, and multiply the original egg plus yogurt weight by 1.5 for your precise amount of flour to use with that specific egg.

STEAMED SAUERKRAUT MANTI

This style of dumpling comes from many countries including Turkey, Armenia, and Afghanistan. Traditionally stuffed with meat, these are instead stuffed with sauerkraut, feta, and onion. These dumplings are easy to make but they do require extra time to prepare.

FOR DOUGH:

230 grams (1¾ cups) all-purpose flour

80 grams (⅓ cup) water

1 large egg

Cabbage leaves for bamboo steamer (optional)

FOR FILLING:

250 grams (1½ cups) sauerkraut (see Chapter 2)

200 grams (1 cup) Feta (see Chapter 3)

100 grams (½ cup) Fermented Red Onions (see Chapter 2)

Black pepper to taste

FOR SAUCE:

120 grams (½ cup) Smen or butter (see Chapter 3)

2 cloves garlic, minced or crushed

40 grams (2 tablespoons) Cultured Whipped Cream (see Chapter 3)

1. Combine flour, water, and egg in a bowl and knead for 2 minutes. Cover dough with a damp cloth or plastic wrap and rest for at least 30 minutes and up to 3 hours.

2. Combine sauerkraut, feta, fermented red onion, and black pepper in a bowl and stir together.

3. Roll out dough as thinly as possible by hand, or use a pasta machine, and then cut into 3" squares.

4. Fill each square with 1–2 scoops of filling. Close by pinching and folding corners together.

5. Line a bamboo steamer with cabbage leaves to prevent manti from sticking. If using a metal steamer, coat the inside with butter.

6. Place manti into steamer baskets and make certain that they do not touch one another. Steam for 40 minutes.

7. In a saucepan, heat the butter over medium heat until melted. Remove from heat and add garlic.

8. Remove manti from steamer and position in circles on serving plates. Place a dollop of cultured cream in the center of each circle. Drizzle each plate with garlic butter sauce and serve.

Short on Time?

Instead of traditional steaming, it is possible to achieve similar results by placing a bamboo steamer basket inside of a large pressure cooker and cooking at 15 PSI for 15 minutes.

YIELD: 2 SERVINGS

🕐 **PREP:** 5 minutes

⭕ **READY IN:** 20 minutes

BACON GREASE TEMPEH

Tempeh isn't just for vegetarians. Fry some up in bacon grease or lard and you will be a tempeh convert too. Serve it with rice or eat it for breakfast with a side of hash browns.

50 grams (4 tablespoons) bacon grease, lard, or cooking oil

1 block Chickpea and Wild Rice Tempeh, cut into 1" strips (see Chapter 5)

Salt

1. Preheat pan on medium-high heat and then add bacon grease.

2. Once bacon grease is hot, add tempeh strips to the pan. Fry on each side for 3–6 minutes until browned and crispy.

3. Remove from pan, salt, and save remaining grease for future use. Serve tempeh warm.

Chapter 8

BREADS

The majority of the bread recipes that follow are for sourdough bread. When I think fermented bread, I think sourdough. In reality, all yeast-leavened bread is fermented whether using commercial yeast or a home-grown sourdough starter.

I didn't include any instant yeast recipes because my preference is to always use a wild ferment if it's available and will work. Some ferments, such as cheese, don't always lend themselves well to a wild or non-laboratory-derived starter culture.

Given that sourdough starter is so easy to make and adds way more complexity to finished breads, I no longer use instant yeast as a leavening agent. If I'm pressed for time, I make something other than bread.

I love all forms of fermentation, so if you are an instant yeast lover, I mean you no ill will by excluding your kind of bread recipes. But if you've never worked with a sourdough culture, you may be surprised at how easy it is, and you might ditch the instant, too.

YIELD: 16 ROLLS

🕐 **PREP:** 30 minutes
⏱ **READY IN:** 12–24 hours

YOGURT AND SOURDOUGH ROLLS

You'll be rolling in the sourdough once you make these rolls. I like to think of them as miniature loaves of bread that are fluffier, sweeter, and that stay fresher a little longer than their larger counterpart. Make them for breakfast, lunch, and dinner, and be sure to use them for Kimcheese Burgers (see Chapter 10).

300 grams (1½ cups) + 400 grams (2½ cups) bread flour

425 grams (2 cups) mesophilic yogurt

250 grams (1 cup) Sourdough Starter (see Chapter 4)

28 grams (2 tablespoons) sugar

1 large egg

50 grams (2 tablespoons) melted butter or olive oil

12 grams (2 teaspoons) salt

Yogurt for wash (optional)

1. The night before you plan to bake these rolls, combine 300 grams bread flour, yogurt, sourdough starter, and sugar in a bowl. The batter will be wet. Cover until the following morning or for at least 8 hours.

2. The following morning, combine the remaining bread flour, egg, butter, and salt with the previous day's batter. Flour hands and work surface and knead by hand for 5–10 minutes. Place dough in a bowl, cover with plastic wrap or a wet cloth, and leave to sit for at least 3 hours and up to 8 hours.

3. Divide dough into 16 balls and place on a pan lined with parchment paper. Cover dough balls with plastic wrap or a wet cloth. Leave to sit for 1–3 hours, or until balls have nearly doubled in size.

4. Preheat oven to 425°F (218°C). Once oven is preheated, uncover the dough balls and brush each ball with yogurt, if desired.

5. Place pan of dough balls into preheated oven and bake for 24–28 minutes.

6. Remove from oven and place rolls on a cooling rack for at least 30 minutes.

Dessert Rolls

Slice these rolls and then toast them with a chocolate bar or chocolate chips in the center for a mildly sweet and delicious dessert. Hazelnut and chocolate spread works too.

KEFIR PRETZELS

These kefir and sourdough pretzels will put a smile on your face. The creaminess of fermented dairy pairs well with the whole wheat and sourdough flavors. There is something simply satisfying about rolling out and twisting pretzels. At first pretzels look difficult to form, but the secret is that they are so simple a baby microbe could do it if only microbes had hands.

400 grams (2¼ cups) bread flour

400 grams (2¼ cups) whole wheat flour

500 grams (2 cups) Sourdough Starter (see Chapter 4)

226 grams (1 cup) Kefir or mesophilic yogurt (see Chapter 3)

42 grams (3 tablespoons) butter, melted

44 grams (2 tablespoons) malt syrup

15 grams (1 tablespoon) salt

1900 grams (8 cups) water

76 grams (2½ tablespoons) baking soda

Flake or kosher salt for topping (Maldon sea salt recommended)

1. Combine flour, sourdough starter, kefir, butter, malt syrup, and salt in a bowl. Knead in bowl for 3–5 minutes. This is a dense and dry dough and so may take some time before fully coming together.

2. Cover and rest dough for at least 30 minutes and up to 3 hours.

3. Knead dough for 10–15 minutes.

4. Cover with plastic wrap or a wet towel and let rest for at least 4 hours and up to 24 hours depending on ambient temperature and desired sourness of final pretzel.

5. Preheat oven to 450°F (232°C) and bring a pot with water and baking soda to a rolling boil.

6. Separate dough into 16 pieces for medium-size pretzels. Roll each dough piece into a cylinder roughly 20" in length and twist into a traditional pretzel shape.

7. Once all pretzels are shaped, place 1–2 pretzels at a time into the boiling water and baking soda solution for 30 seconds. Remove each pretzel with a slotted spoon and place on a parchment-lined pan. Top each pretzel with flake or kosher salt.

8. Bake pretzels in oven for 18–20 minutes, or until a deep golden-brown color. Place on cooling rack and allow to cool for at least 30 minutes.

YIELD:
5 BELGIAN WAFFLES
OR 8 PANCAKES

🕐 **PREP:** 10 minutes

🫙 **FERMENTATION:**
12–24 hours

SOURDOUGH BELGIAN WAFFLES

Want light, fluffy, and crispy Belgian-style waffles, but don't feel like whipping egg into white peaks early in the morning? Then let the power of sourdough do the heavy lifting for you. When you're feeding your sourdough starter, instead of discarding the extra, mix it up in the evening and you will be prepared for beautiful waffles the following morning. Any sourdough starter will work; I've used white, whole wheat, rye, and even old and very sour starter. Each type of sourdough tastes unique but all perform equally well.

This recipe also works for pancakes but you may need to add more kefir if the batter is too thick.

240 grams (2 cups) flour

240 grams (1 cup) Sourdough Starter (see Chapter 4)

400 grams (1½ cups) Kefir or mesophilic yogurt (see Chapter 3)

25 grams (2 tablespoons) sugar

2 large eggs

50 grams (3½ tablespoons) melted butter or coconut oil

7 grams (1 teaspoon) salt

5 grams (1 teaspoon) baking soda

1. At least 6 hours before you plan to make waffles, mix the flour, sourdough starter, kefir, and sugar in a bowl. Cover with cloth or plastic wrap and allow to ferment for at least 6 hours or overnight.

2. When ready to make waffles, preheat waffle maker.

3. Mix the eggs, butter, salt, and baking soda in a separate bowl.

4. Stir in the previous day's ferment until just combined.

5. Pour batter into waffle maker and cook until desired color is reached.

6. In order to remain crispy, leave waffles on a wire rack until ready to serve.

7. Bonus: If you double or triple this recipe, you can freeze extras. Slightly undercook each waffle and then freeze. When ready to eat, put them back into a waffle maker to crisp and warm.

CHAPTER 9

SOUPS, STEWS, AND SALADS

It's easy to add fermented foods to soups, stews, and salads. Just toss anything in and stir it around. But if you're interested in trying a few dishes that highlight specific ferments then be sure to try the following recipes. They can fulfill a fermented craving for any mood or occasion.

SRIRACHA CABBAGE SALAD

This rich and cold salad is a refreshing summer treat but I enjoy it so much that I eat it throughout the winter as well. This is one recipe where I do not use specific proportions. Add as much Sriracha sauce as you can handle and make sure you add enough mayonnaise to coat the vegetables.

Sriracha sauce

Mayonnaise

Blankimchi (see Chapter 2)

1. Mix Sriracha sauce and mayonnaise in bowl with the fermented napa cabbage and carrots.

2. Serve immediately.

TOMATO AND YOGURT SOUP

This is a warm, semi-thick, and filling soup that is wonderfully comforting on a cold winter day. Serve as a light meal or in smaller portions as a starter.

40 grams (2½ tablespoons) butter

1 medium onion, finely chopped

480 grams (2 cups) yogurt (see Chapter 3)

240 grams (1 cup) water

80 grams (⅓ cup) tomatoes, pureed

10 grams (1 tablespoon) tapioca flour

0.5 grams (½ teaspoon) salt

3 cloves garlic, minced

0.5 grams (1 teaspoon) oregano

2 large eggs, beaten

85 grams (½ cup) rice, cooked

1. Melt butter in a pot over medium-low heat. Add onions and sauté until golden brown.

2. While onions are cooking, combine yogurt, water, tomatoes, tapioca flour, and salt in a bowl and whisk together.

3. Once onions are browned, add garlic to the pot and cook for 30 seconds.

4. Add the contents of the bowl to the pot and bring to a boil stirring constantly. Simmer for 10 minutes. Add oregano and simmer for an additional 5 minutes, stirring occasionally.

5. Combine eggs and a few spoonfuls of the hot soup in a bowl and immediately whisk together. Then add egg mixture to the pot and gently stir. Simmer for 3 more minutes.

6. Split the cooked rice between soup bowls, creating a small mound of rice in each bowl. Ladle soup onto the rice and serve immediately.

MISO AND MUSHROOM SOUP

This flavorful soup has umami action coming from both the mushrooms and miso. Double the recipe and add noodles or tempeh for a full meal, or enjoy as an accompaniment to a main course as is.

7 grams (½ tablespoon) butter or oil

10 grams (1 tablespoon) Fermented Red Onions (see Chapter 2)

4 shiitake mushrooms, thinly sliced

480 grams (2 cups) water

50 grams (3 tablespoons) Sweet White Miso (see Chapter 5)

25 grams (2 tablespoons) Spicy Dill Carrots (see Chapter 2)

15 grams (½ cup) watercress, chopped

1. In a saucepan, melt butter over medium-low heat. Add fermented onions and sauté on medium-high heat for 2 minutes. Note that fermented onions cook much quicker than fresh so don't overcook.

2. Add mushrooms and sauté along with the onions until lightly browned, about 2 minutes.

3. Combine 100 grams (½ cup) of the water and miso in a small bowl and whisk together until miso is dissolved.

4. Add the remaining water to the saucepan and heat to a gentle simmer. Add miso, carrots, and watercress.

5. Once the soup returns to a simmer, remove from heat and serve.

ALTERNATIVE USES FOR MISO

Have miso and a desire to venture beyond soups? Try making a creamy miso dressing or use miso as a glaze on roasted vegetables. Or go sweet by adding miso to muffins, brownies, or even miso-flavored ice cream. Spread the miso love to all foods.

POLISH PORK AND SAUERKRAUT STEW

YIELD: 8 SERVINGS

🕐 **PREP:** 40 minutes
◯ **READY IN:** 4 hours

Also known as bigos, this style of recipe uses a lot of sauerkraut and meat. The sauerkraut goes so well with the pork that it is worth the effort of making extra sauerkraut. It is also a great way to use sauerkraut that has aged past its prime.

Interested in a meat-free bigos? Fried tempeh is a reasonable alternative in this stew. Or add the fried tempeh along with the pork.

24 grams (2 tablespoons) clarified butter, oil, or lard

450 grams (1 pound) Canadian bacon, sliced

1 large onion, chopped

1 small cabbage, thinly sliced

14 grams (1 tablespoon) fish sauce

230 grams (1 cup) red wine

240 grams (1 cup) water

790 grams (3⅓ cups) canned tomatoes and juice, chopped

450 grams (3 cups) sauerkraut (see Chapter 2)

4 cloves garlic, minced

450 grams (1 pound) kielbasa, sliced into ½" rounds

Cultured Whipped Cream or strained yogurt (see Chapter 3)

Black pepper

1. Melt clarified butter in a large pot over medium-high heat. Add Canadian bacon and fry until browned and partially crispy. Remove from pot and reserve for later.

2. Add onions, cabbage, and fish sauce to the pot and cook on medium for about 15–20 minutes. Cabbage will shrink and onions will begin to brown.

3. Add the red wine, water, tomatoes, sauerkraut, and garlic. Bring to a boil and then lower heat to simmer for 2 hours.

4. Add Canadian bacon and kielbasa and simmer for 30 minutes.

5. May be served immediately with a dollop of cultured cream and black pepper to taste. The flavors will continue to meld if refrigerated and so may also be reheated over the next week with great success.

SLOW COOKER?

The first time I tried making a bigos, it was in a slow cooker. This was a mistake. Some of the ingredients need to be cooked at different temperatures in the beginning in order for everything to taste as it should. I still use a slow cooker on high for the 2-hour simmer but only to reserve stovetop space.

KOMBUCHA APPLE SALAD

Sweet apple and sour kombucha make for a refreshing late summer or early fall salad. If you forget to bottle your kombucha before it gets too sour, then start making this dressing and eventually you will use it all up.

Note that this dressing must be used immediately, otherwise the smen will solidify. For an interesting side effect, toss the dressing and then chill before serving for a perfectly coated salad with dressing that won't collect in the bottom of a bowl.

FOR DRESSING:

35 grams (1¼ tablespoons) Smen, melted (see Chapter 3)

10 grams (2 teaspoons) Kombucha, aged and sour (see Chapter 6)

8 grams (1 teaspoon) ginger simple syrup (see Chapter 11, Pickled and Candied Ginger)

4 grams (1 teaspoon) Kefir or yogurt (see Chapter 3)

FOR SALAD:

Salad greens

1 apple, julienned or diced

Large handful walnuts, chopped

Handful raisins

1. Combine smen, kombucha, simple syrup, and kefir in a bowl and whisk until emulsified.

2. Combine salad greens, apple, walnuts, and raisins in a large bowl, add salad dressing.

3. Toss, plate, and serve.

MASON JAR BLENDER

Don't feel like whisking the salad dressing by hand? Then fill a Mason jar with the ingredients and screw it onto the bottom attachment of a regular blender and blend away.

CHAPTER 10

PIZZAS AND SANDWICHES

Don't know what to do with this or that ferment? Slap it on a pizza or sandwich and you've got yourself a full meal. Ferment the pizza or bread dough and you may end up eating a 100% fermented meal. Sandwiches and pizzas are second only to rice and pastas as my favorite ways to consume fermented foods.

While pizzas and sandwiches are similar food items in my mind, the act of using fermented food ingredients separates them in one distinct way: Pizzas cook the ferments and sandwiches leave most of the ferments raw. If eating more live cultures is your number-one priority, you may lean towards the sandwiches in this section. Otherwise, if it is all about flavor, go wild with both.

SAUERKRAUT PRETZEL GRILLED CHEESE

This soft sourdough pretzel with melted cheese and warm sauerkraut makes for an excellent lunch. Add sliced meat, such as bratwurst, for a more intensely German vibe.

1 Kefir Pretzel (see Chapter 8)

Cheese

Sauerkraut (see Chapter 2)

28 grams (2 tablespoons) butter

1. Slice pretzel in half and layer each side with cheese and sandwich together with sauerkraut in the center.

2. Melt butter in a pan on medium low. Add the pretzel sandwich to the pan and cover. Grill until cheese begins to melt. Turn over, and grill for 2–3 more minutes.

3. Serve hot.

Toaster Oven Cheese

It takes a bit of practice to master melting and flipping pretzel sandwiches in a pan. So it may not be a grilled cheese anymore, but you can make a tasty sandwich using these same ingredients in a toaster oven. Melt the cheese onto both inner sides of the pretzel. Then add the sauerkraut and sandwich it all together.

🕐 **PREP:** 20 minutes

🫙 **FERMENTATION:** 1–2 days

SOURDOUGH PIZZA DOUGH

Once you realize how simple it is to make pizza dough at home, don't be surprised if you start eating a lot more pizza. This thin-crust recipe goes so well with fermented toppings that you may soon be fermenting certain vegetables exclusively for pizza.

You will need a cast-iron pizza pan, pizza stone, or a large landscaping stone in order to bake these thin-crust pizzas in your oven at its highest setting. My preference is a cast-iron pizza pan because it takes less time to preheat and it holds heat well. For a less expensive option, large landscaping stones work great and are less likely to break compared with thinner pizza stones. You can find landscaping stones at your local hardware or gardening store.

275 grams (2 cups) all-purpose flour

12 grams (½ tablespoon) salt

165 grams (½ cup) water

104 grams (⅓ cup) Sourdough Starter (see Chapter 4)

10 grams (2 teaspoons) olive oil

1. Combine all ingredients in a large bowl. Mix with hands until all ingredients come together. Cover and rest dough for at least 30 minutes and up to 3 hours.

2. Knead dough on a floured surfaced for 3–5 minutes.

3. Divide dough into 2 balls, wrap tightly in plastic, and refrigerate for at least 6 and up to 48 hours.

4. When ready to use, remove pizza dough from refrigerator and allow to warm to room temperature before shaping.

WHOLE WHEAT VERSION

It won't taste like a traditional pizza crust, but this same recipe can be used with whole wheat bread flour instead of white flour. The difference? The pizza will taste more like a cracker and the crust will be crispier.

KIMCHI PIZZA

Is there anything that kimchi doesn't taste good in or on? This pizza tastes especially good with the addition of goat cheese but it is the kimchi that's amore.

YIELD: 14" PIZZA

🕐 **PREP:** 10 minutes
◯ **READY IN:** 20 minutes

1 Sourdough Pizza Dough ball
(see previous recipe)

40 grams (2½ tablespoons) tomatoes,
pureed

20 grams (1 tablespoon) goat cheese

10 grams (½ tablespoon) Sweet White
Miso (see Chapter 5)

60 grams (2 tablespoons) Red Kimchi
(see Chapter 2)

70 grams (¼ cup) mozzarella, torn

Flour for work surface and pizza peel

1. Remove pizza dough from refrigerator (if applicable) and allow to warm to room temperature.

2. Preheat oven and cast-iron pizza pan or pizza stone to 550°F (288°C) or your oven's highest setting.

3. Combine tomatoes, goat cheese, and miso in a small bowl and stir until smooth.

4. Gently sift a small amount of flour across pizza peel. As an alternative to a pizza peel, the backside of a cookie sheet will work nearly as well.

5. Flour work surface and gently press the pizza dough into a flat round shape with fingertips.

6. Pick up dough and using gravity to shape the pizza, toss the flat dough from one hand to the other. Dough will begin to sag. The key is to get the dough to sag where you want it. With each toss, turn the dough a quarter of a turn to create a round pizza (it will still taste great even if a little lopsided).

7. Gently place the shaped pizza dough on floured pizza peel. Work fast when laying down the dough and applying toppings so as to prevent the dough from sticking to the pizza peel. The longer it sits, the harder it will be to transfer to the oven, and the more likely that the pizza will be damaged in the process.

8. Apply the tomato, goat cheese, and miso sauce to the pizza with circular motions using the back of a large spoon.

9. Drop kimchi on pizza and then top with torn chunks of mozzarella.

10. Immediately transfer pizza from peel to oven and bake for 6–10 minutes.

11. Remove from oven and transfer to a cutting board. Allow to cool for 1 minute before slicing.

🕐 **PREP:** 10 minutes

🕐 **READY IN:** 20 minutes

FETA AND PEPPERONI PIZZA

You may not have fermented the pepperoni yourself, but it still counts as a fermented pizza topping. You did make the feta though, didn't you? While you're at it, you should try fermenting your own banana peppers.

1 Sourdough Pizza Dough ball (see recipe in this chapter)

45 grams (3 tablespoons) tomatoes, pureed

10 grams (½ tablespoon) olive oil

20 small pepperoni, thinly sliced

30 grams (3 tablespoons) banana peppers

90 grams (½ cup) Feta, diced or crumbled (see Chapter 3)

Flour for work surface and pizza peel

1. Remove pizza dough from refrigerator (if applicable) and allow to warm to room temperature.

2. Preheat oven and cast-iron pizza pan or pizza stone to 550°F (288°C) or your oven's highest setting.

3. Gently sift a small amount of flour across pizza peel.

4. Flour work surface and gently press the pizza dough into a flat round shape with fingertips.

5. Pick up dough and using gravity to shape the pizza, toss the flat dough from one hand to the other. With each toss, turn the dough a quarter of a turn to create a round pizza.

6. Gently place the shaped pizza dough on floured pizza peel.

7. Apply the pureed tomatoes to the pizza with circular motions using the back of a large spoon. Sprinkle olive oil on top.

8. Distribute pepperoni slices evenly across pizza.

9. Scatter banana peppers over pizza and top with feta cheese.

10. Immediately transfer pizza from peel to oven and bake for 6–10 minutes.

11. Remove from oven and transfer to cutting board. Allow to cool for 1 minute before slicing.

KIMCHEESE BURGER

There is kimchi flavor inside and out of this burger with melted mozzarella cheese holding everything in place. This could also be called a 5-ferment burger, but who's counting?

454 grams (1 pound) ground beef, 85%

7 grams (1 tablespoon) Korean red pepper powder

6 grams (1 teaspoon) salt

1 gram (¼ teaspoon) ginger powder

1 gram (¼ teaspoon) onion powder

1 gram (¼ teaspoon) garlic powder

Red Kimchi (see Chapter 2)

Mozzarella cheese, torn or sliced

Fermented Red Onions (see Chapter 2)

1 cucumber pickle, sliced

4 Yogurt and Sourdough Rolls, halved (see Chapter 8)

1. Combine ground beef, red pepper powder, salt, ground ginger, onion powder, and garlic powder in a bowl.

2. Separate and form ground beef into 6-8 hamburger patties.

3. Grill to your liking, topping with kimchi and torn mozzarella after flipping burgers. Alternatively, once grilled, place hamburger under a broiler or heat lamp in order to melt cheese.

4. Remove from grill and top with fermented onion and pickle.

5. Sandwich each burger between 2 halves of sourdough roll and serve immediately.

FERMENT DOG

This dog packs a fermentation punch. If you're going to eat a hot dog instead of a fermented sausage, then you might as well pile on a few ferments to make up for it. This hot dog is a beauty, but be prepared for a messy mouthful in every bite.

118 grams (½ cup) water

60 grams (¼ cup) soy sauce

25 grams (2 tablespoons) fish sauce

8 hot dogs

Yogurt and Sourdough Rolls shaped as hot dog buns (see Chapter 8)

Mayonnaise

Sauerkraut (see Chapter 2)

Fermented Red Onions (see Chapter 2)

Red Kimchi (see Chapter 2)

Cucumber pickles, diced

1. Combine water, soy sauce, and fish sauce in a sealable container.

2. Poke holes into each hot dog with a fork or other utensil and marinate in soy and fish sauce for at least 12 hours in the refrigerator.

3. Grill hot dogs to your liking.

4. Slice sourdough bun and spread each inner side with a thin layer of mayonnaise.

5. Insert hot dog into bun and top with layers of sauerkraut, fermented onions, kimchi, and cucumber pickles.

6. Serve with plenty of napkins.

MUFFULETTA SANDWICH

This sandwich uses fermented giardiniera, but it is missing the olives. If you really can't enjoy a muffuletta sandwich without olives, dice a few up and add them to the giardiniera before making your sandwich. Either way, get ready for a giant sandwich packed with meat, cheese, and fermented vegetables. Note: Preparation time for this recipe does not include fermenting and baking the bread.

Yogurt and Sourdough Rolls dough recipe (see Chapter 8)

Sesame seeds

Giardiniera (see Chapter 2), diced

Salami, sliced

Large pepperoni, sliced

Mozzarella, sliced

Green olives, diced (optional)

1. Use the full recipe for the Yogurt and Sourdough Rolls (see Chapter 8) and shape into one large loaf. Gently flatten into a disk and cover with plastic wrap for at least 1 hour or until doubled in size.

2. Brush with yogurt wash, top with sesame seeds, and bake on a pan lined with parchment at 400°F (204°C) for 28–32 minutes.

3. Once bread is cool, slice in half horizontally. Spread giardiniera on the top half.

4. Sandwich layers of salami, pepperoni, and mozzarella between the bread halves. Add olives, if using.

5. Slice muffuletta sandwich into individual servings, pizza or pie style. Serve immediately or refrigerate until ready to use in order to allow flavors to mingle.

PB&K

Who needs jelly when you can eat spicy kimchi instead? If you think cucumber pickles and peanut butter make a good combination, then you are about to be amazed by peanut butter and kimchi. Serve as a sandwich or cut into fourths for use as a first course.

Peanut butter

Sourdough bread, sliced

Red Kimchi (see Chapter 2)

1. Spread a moderate layer of peanut butter on the inside of bread slices.

2. Sandwich a small amount of kimchi between the bread and peanut butter.

3. Cut into sections or serve whole.

SUBSTITUTIONS

Why stop at kimchi? Why not try PB&S(auerkraut) or PB&T(empeh)? And no one says jelly can't join back in on the fun. Strained yogurt and jelly sandwich, anyone?

KIMCHI PORK BUREK

Kimchi and ground pork belong together. Add some taco-esque (a.k.a. kimch-aco) seasoning and the crunch of crispy phyllo pastry and you have yourself an exciting meal that works equally well on the go or as a sit-down affair.

Note that if you do not wish to roll your own phyllo dough, you can purchase it in the freezer section of most grocery stores.

(continued on following page)

YIELD: 4–6 SERVINGS

PREP: 45 minutes

READY IN: 2–10 hours

FOR PHYLLO DOUGH:

385 grams (3 cups) all-purpose flour

18 grams (1½ tablespoons) vinegar

8 grams (½ tablespoon) olive oil

165 grams (⅔ cup) warm water

Olive oil or melted butter, for brushing

FOR KIMCH-ACO SEASONING:

10 grams (1 tablespoon) chili powder

3 grams (½ teaspoon) salt

2 grams (1 teaspoon) black pepper, ground

2 grams (1 teaspoon) Korean coarse red pepper

1 gram (½ teaspoon) garlic powder

1 gram (½ teaspoon) onion powder

FOR KIMCHI AND PORK FILLING:

450 grams (1 pound) ground pork

300 grams (2 cups) Red Kimchi (see Chapter 2)

1. Place flour in a bowl and make a well. Add vinegar and oil to the well and combine with flour by hand. Add warm water and knead until combined.

2. Let dough rest for at least 30 minutes or preferably up to 8 hours before use.

3. Combine chili powder, salt, black pepper, red pepper, garlic powder, and onion powder in a bowl and whisk together.

4. Combine ground pork, kimchi, and kimch-aco seasoning in a bowl and massage with hands until just blended. Do not overwork the pork.

5. Preheat a pan over medium-high heat. Add pork filling and cook for 5–10 minutes, until lightly browned, stirring occasionally.

6. Preheat oven to 350°F (176°C) and oil a large cast-iron skillet. Note: If cast iron is not an option, a glass square cake pan or other bakeware can be used.

7. Separate dough into smaller sections and roll out by hand or use a pasta machine to roll dough until paper-thin and translucent. If rolling by hand, cut into 6"-wide sections. If using a pasta machine, each rolled piece of dough will already be the proper width. Use whatever length you feel comfortable working with as the ends will be connected in the pan.

8. Lightly brush oil on one length of rolled phyllo dough. Gently layer 2 more phyllo dough sheets on top, applying oil on each sheet before stacking.

9. Spoon a 1"-thick line of pork filling along one of the long edges of the stacked sheets. Gently roll the filling and phyllo dough into a tube.

10. Starting in the center of the cast-iron pan, wrap the tube into a spiral. Repeat with remaining sheets and filling, connecting each new tube to the last with a slight pinch and tuck.

11. When spiral round is complete, brush lightly with oil.

12. Bake for 35–40 minutes or until phyllo turns golden brown. Allow to cool for 15 minutes before slicing like a pie and serving.

ALTERNATIVE FILLINGS

Other ideas for fillings are cheese and sauerkraut or ground beef and fermented onions. Try them all and then invent your own.

CHAPTER 11

DESSERTS, SWEETS, AND SNACKS

You've eaten healthy through this entire cook-book, but now it's time for some fermented junk food. I'm of the mindset that if I'm going to eat sweets and snacks, at least they're probably healthier if I make them at home.

Health aside, these sweets and snacks just taste delicious. Most of them involve yogurt or cultured cream, which is an ideal candidate for desserts. In addition, there are a few funky recipes, like Pickled and Candied Ginger that is even more exciting on the tongue than regular crystallized ginger. And don't forget to try the Peanut Butter and Sauerkraut Cream Cookies. The sauerkraut is subtle but goes well served with an after-dinner beer.

🕐 **PREP:** 30 minutes

🫙 **FERMENTATION:** 3-6 weeks

🧂 **SALT:** 5%

PICKLED AND CANDIED GINGER

I love crystallized ginger; it's the only candy that I'll readily eat. This fermented version is meatier, saltier, and more flavorful than the nonfermented variety. The usual step of boiling the ginger in water before adding to simple syrup is skipped since most of the tough ginger fibers are softened during the 3-6 week fermentation.

450 grams (4½ cups) ginger, peeled and thinly sliced

350 grams (1½ cups) water

18 grams (1½ tablespoons) salt

400 grams (2 cups) sugar + extra for coating (optional)

470 grams (2 cups) water

1. Add the ginger, water, and salt into a pint-size jar. Close lid and shake until salt dissolves. Leave to ferment, away from direct sunlight, for 3-6 weeks. Release any pressure that builds up over the first week by quickly opening and closing the lid.

2. Strain away the brine from the fermented ginger.

3. Add ginger, sugar, and water to a pot and heat on high, stirring frequently, until reaching 225°F (107°C), or until sugar and water thicken and turn golden in color, about 20-30 minutes.

4. Remove from heat and let cool for 10 minutes. Strain through sieve and save the ginger-infused simple syrup for other uses such as flavoring for the second stage of kombucha fermentation (see Chapter 6).

5. Immediately toss candied ginger in sugar while still hot and wet (optional).

6. Enjoy immediately or leave to dry on a cooling rack for at least 12 hours before storing.

Candied Carrots

If you develop a sweet tooth for pickled and candied vegetables, then give pickled carrots a try too. Sliced into whatever shape you desire, carrots only require a 1-2 week fermentation before they are ready to be cooked in sugar. They work great as topping on a fermented carrot cake.

SOUR CABBAGE CRISPS

Fermentation, like dehydration, is a form of food preservation. The idea of doing both may seem like overkill. How overpreserved can a food get? But there are many cultures that ferment foods, dry them, and then grind them into a flour. Cassava is a good example of this. Fermentation is sometimes the first step to making a food edible and dehydration is what preserves or alters it into a ready-to-cook form.

Yet, preservation is not the goal of this recipe. This is an experiment in taste and the transformation of dehydration. When drying sauerkraut in a dehydrator, the biggest challenge is to produce a crispy product as opposed to a leathery or chewy one. Electric home dehydrators and the ambient humidity surrounding them can make for inconsistent results. If your crisps don't turn out crispy, try dehydrating for longer or at a higher temperature.

Sauerkraut (see Chapter 2)

1. Press or squeeze out as much juice as possible from the sauerkraut.

2. Place sauerkraut onto dehydrator trays.

3. Dehydrate for 6–24 hours at 125°F (50°C), until dry and crispy.

4. Bonus: Grind the crisps into powder and use as a seasoning or spice.

Kimchi Spice

Try this same recipe with kimchi and once dehydrated, use a pestle and mortar or spice grinder to grind the kimchi into a powder. Instant spicy umami seasoning!

BERRY KEFIR LEATHER

Transform kefir and fruit into a
chewy snack. Use a mild kefir unless
you like to pucker (dehydration
enhances the sour flavor). For
even faster preparation, you can
substitute the fruit and sugar with
premade jelly or fruit preserves.

500 grams (2 cups) Kefir or yogurt (see Chapter 3)

120 grams (1 cup) frozen berries

10 grams (1 tablespoon) sugar

4 grams (1 teaspoon) vanilla extract

1. Blend all ingredients together in a blender or food processor until smooth.

2. Line 2 dehydrator trays with plastic wrap, parchment paper, or silicone mats.

3. Pour and divide blended ingredients between the 2 trays.

4. Dehydrate at 125°F (57°C) for 4–8 hours. Kefir leather should peel away easily and not be overly sticky.

5. Slice or cut kefir leather into desired shapes.

CHOCOLATE BERRY CULTURED ICE CREAM

Want to make creamy and smooth ice cream but don't have an ice cream maker? This recipe uses a freezer and food processor instead. Do you love the taste of ice cream but are lactose intolerant? This recipe uses cultured cream so microbes have already digested most of the lactose.

500 grams (2 cups) Cultured Whipped Cream (see Chapter 3)

225 grams (1 cup) sugar

185 grams (¾ cup) Kefir or yogurt (see Chapter 3)

14 grams (1 tablespoon) vanilla extract

100 grams (½ cup) semi-sweet chocolate chips

240 grams (2 cups) frozen blackberries

1. Combine cultured cream, sugar, kefir, and vanilla extract in a plastic freezer bag. Massage the bag gently to mix. Lie flat in freezer and leave until frozen solid. Depending on freezer and original temperature of ingredients, this may take anywhere from 4–10 hours.

2. Pulse chocolate chips in food processor until broken into tiny pieces. Remove from food processor and set aside.

3. Blend frozen blackberries in food processor until smooth.

4. Once cream is frozen, break or cut the frozen mass into pieces that will fit inside the food processor. Add to food processor and blend with berries until smooth. It may be necessary to cut or break frozen chunks into smaller pieces if they are not fully blending.

5. Add chocolate pieces and pulse in food processor for a few seconds until combined.

6. If thicker cultured ice cream is desired, return to freezer for another 2–6 hours before serving.

Alternative Flavors

Replace the blackberries and chocolate with anything you desire.
Think salted caramel, sourdough cookie dough, or even fermented
fruit. Some experimentation with ingredients and quantities may
be necessary to obtain the same consistency, but even a cultured
ice cream experiment gone wrong will still taste good!

🕐 **PREP:** 30 minutes
◎ **READY IN:** 1 hour

PEANUT BUTTER AND SAUERKRAUT CREAM COOKIES

Weird, savory, and sweet this combination may be, but delicious indeed.

FOR PEANUT BUTTER COOKIE:

140 grams (½ cup) peanut butter

130 grams (½ cup) brown sugar

110 grams (½ cup) butter, softened

1 large egg

4 grams (½ teaspoon) vanilla extract

225 grams (1½ cups) all-purpose flour

5 grams (½ teaspoon) salt

0.5 grams (1 teaspoon) baking soda

FOR SAUERKRAUT CREAM FILLING:

130 grams (¾ cup) Cultured Whipped Cream (see Chapter 3)

50 grams (½ cup) sauerkraut (see Chapter 2)

1. Combine peanut butter, brown sugar, butter, egg, and vanilla extract in a bowl. Mix until thoroughly blended.

2. Combine flour, salt, and baking soda in a separate bowl. Whisk until blended.

3. Add dry ingredients to wet and mix until smooth.

4. Separate into small balls approximately 30 grams (2 tablespoons) each. Freeze cookie dough balls for 30 minutes.

5. Preheat oven to 350°F (177°C).

6. In a blender or food processor, blend together cultured cream and sauerkraut until relatively smooth. Chill in refrigerator until ready to use.

7. Remove cookie dough from freezer and press each ball into a flat circle. Place on an ungreased cookie sheet and bake for 8–12 minutes.

8. Remove from oven and rest for 10 minutes on cookie sheet.

9. Place a small amount of cream filling on the top of one cookie. Press another cookie on top of the cream to create a sandwich. There is no need to spread the cream as it will press out to the sides during the process. Repeat for all cookies.

10. Serve warm or chilled.

FERMENTED TOASTER PASTRY

Craving the flavors of pie, but not interested in the long wait for it to bake or cool? This recipe is quick and easy to whip up. If you manage to keep from eating them all on the first day, they warm up well in a toaster.

FOR SWEET:

70 grams (½ cup) fresh, frozen, or preserved berries

50 grams (¼ cup) Strained Yogurt (see Chapter 3)

15 grams (1 tablespoon) sugar (optional)

1 Yogurt Pie Crust dough (see recipe in this chapter)

OR

FOR SAVORY:

90 grams (½ cup) Feta, diced or crumbled (see Chapter 3)

30 grams (1 cup) spinach

4 Leek Rings, minced (see Chapter 2)

1 Yogurt Pie Crust dough (see recipe in this chapter)

1. Preheat oven to 350°F (176°C).

2. Combine ingredients for sweet and/or savory fillings until smooth.

3. Lightly dust work surface with flour. Roll out the yogurt pie crust dough until approximately ⅛–¹⁄₁₆" thick. Partition into multiple balls before rolling if working with limited counter space.

4. Cut away edges to form a large square or rectangle. Cut into 3-4 equal columns.

5. Fill half of the column with filling in the center. Fold over the empty half, gently press around the edges with fingers, and then press again with a fork.

6. Poke each pastry with a toothpick, fork, or other sharp utensil at least six times to prevent exploding pastries in the oven.

7. Bake for 20-25 minutes and then cool on a wire rack. Serve as is or toast before serving.

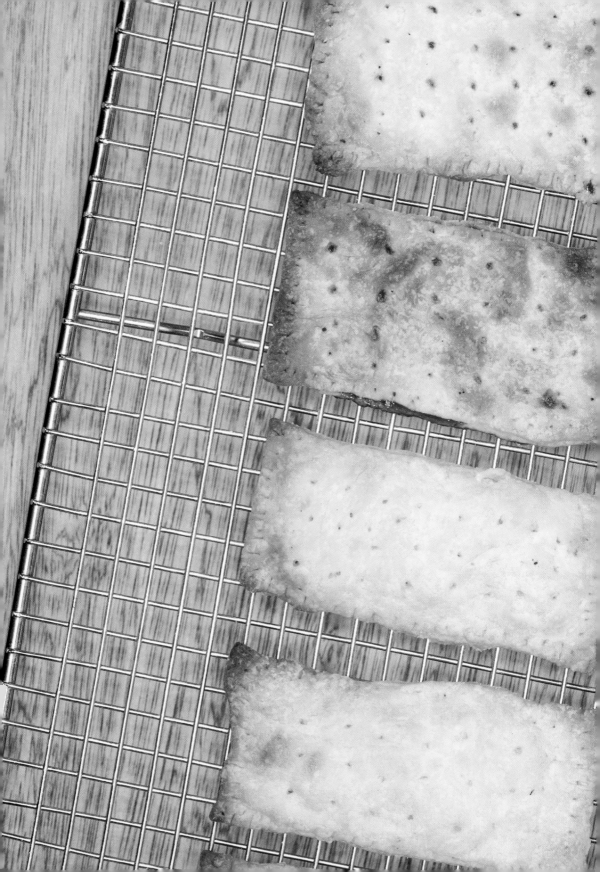

HARD CIDER PIE

Ferment your apples before baking them for an enjoyably complex and flavorful pie. Fermenting the apples is easy. Follow the recipe for making Apple Cider (see Chapter 6) and add at least 3 thinly sliced red apples to the apple juice during the beginning of the process. Apples can be used for pie once wild yeasts have joined the party and the juice is actively bubbling.

For more tartness, allow the apples and cider to ferment beyond alcohol fermentation into just the beginning stages of vinegar fermentation—a sort of cider/vinegar hybrid.

500 grams (about 4) green apples, thinly sliced

225 grams (about 3) fermented apples (see Chapter 6)

125 grams (½ cup) sugar

20 grams (2 tablespoons) flour

2 grams (1 teaspoon) salt

1 gram (¼ teaspoon) cinnamon

1 gram (¼ teaspoon) nutmeg

1 Yogurt Pie Crust dough (see recipe in this chapter)

14 grams (1 tablespoon) butter, diced

1. Preheat oven to 425°F (218°C).

2. Combine green apples, fermented apples, sugar, flour, salt, cinnamon, and nutmeg in a bowl and stir until apples are fully coated with all ingredients.

3. Butter a pie pan.

4. Separate pie crust dough into 2 sections and roll out the first one. Place rolled-out dough into the bottom of the pie pan and press into place.

5. Roll out the second dough section for the top of the pie.

6. Add apple mixture to the pie pan and top with the diced butter. Cover pie with upper pie crust dough and pinch or shape edges in order to seal to your liking.

7. Bake for 15 minutes and then lower oven temperature to 350°F (176°C) for 45 minutes until crust has turned golden brown.

8. Remove from oven and cool for at least 1 hour before serving.

YOGURT PIE CRUST

Why use water when you can bake with yogurt instead? Add in your homemade cultured butter and you've got yourself a pie crust brimming with fermentation. Use this crust for any pie or toaster pastry that you can imagine.

250 grams (2 cups) + 100 grams (¾ cup) all-purpose flour

226 grams (1 cup) cold butter

5 grams (1 teaspoon) salt

130 grams (½ cup) cold yogurt or Kefir (see Chapter 3)

1. Combine 250 grams (2 cups) flour, butter, and salt in a food processor. Pulse until combined into small bits.

2. Add remaining flour and pulse until just combined. Do not over-process.

3. Transfer dough to a bowl. Add some of the yogurt to the bowl and begin to combine with hand or spoon. Continue to add yogurt until the dough comes together in a ball. It may not be necessary to use all of the yogurt.

4. Separate dough into 2 balls. If not using immediately, cover each dough ball in plastic wrap and refrigerate for up to 24 hours.

5. Roll out dough for 1 pie with 2 crusts or for 2 pies with 1 crust.

WHERE DO YOU GO FROM HERE?

This is only the beginning. Fermented foods are, or can be, anywhere. If you ferment it, the flavor will come. As you continue your journey, you are bound to unlock new flavor combinations that you have not yet imagined. This is the beauty of fermented foods.

If your interest has been piqued, you can more deeply explore the fermenting of meat, cheese, and alcohol. Each has vast histories full of culture and tradition. Learn from the past, but after learning the basic skills, don't be afraid to experiment beyond the bounds of authenticity.

New flavors await you and the world. Fermentation is no longer merely an act of preservation. It's about discovering new flavors and cultures. Fermentation isn't just a chore, it is a desirable luxury. Bathe in the brine and inhale the fermenting aromas of your projects as you learn more.

Most important, share your ferments and share your knowledge. These are special skills that should not be relegated to the few. Not everyone will find joy in DIY fermentation, but most have a weakness for a ferment or two. These are fascinating flavors in which we can all partake. Welcome to the world of fermentation and microbial diversity. May microbes, good food, and a burning desire to eat and learn always be with you.

RESOURCES

Starter Culture Suppliers

Cultures for Health—*www.culturesforhealth.com*

GEM Cultures—*www.gemcultures.com*

Dairy Connection—*www.getculture.com*

New England Cheesemaking Supply Company—*www.cheesemaking.com*

The Ginger Beer Plant—*www.gingerbeerplant.net*

Fermentation Reading

Bamforth, Charles W. *Food. Fermentation and Micro-organisms*. (Ames, IA: Blackwell Science, 2005).

Boetticher, Taylor, and Toponia Mille. *In the Charcuterie: The Fatted Calf's Guide to Making Sausage, Salumi, Pates, Roasts, Confits, and Other Meaty Goods*. (Berkeley, CA: Ten Speed Press, 2013).

Caldwell, Gianaclis. *Mastering Artisan Cheesemaking: The Ultimate Guide for Home-Scale and Market Producers*. (White River Junction, VT: Chelsea Green Publishing, 2012).

Christensen, Emma. *True Brews: How to Craft Fermented Cider, Beer, Wine, Sake, Soda, Mead, Kefir, and Kombucha at Home*. (Berkeley, CA: Ten Speed Press, 2013).

Chun, Lauryn. *The Kimchi Cookbook: 60 Traditional and Modern Ways to Make and Eat Kimchi*. (Berkeley, CA: Ten Speed Press, 2012).

Ciciarelli, Jill. *Fermented: A Four Season Approach to Paleo Probiotic Foods*. (Las Vegas, NV: Victory Belt Publishing, 2013).

Davies, Sasha. *The Cheesemaker's Apprentice*. (Beverly, MA: Quarry Books, 2012).

Haroutunian, Arto Der. *The Yogurt Cookbook: Recipes from Around the World*. (Northampton, MA: Interlink Publishing Group, 2013).

Karlin, Mary. *Artisan Cheese Making at Home: Techniques and Recipes for Mastering World-Class Cheeses*. (Berkeley, CA: Ten Speed Press, 2011).

Karlin, Mary. *Mastering Fermentation: Recipes for Making and Cooking with Fermented Foods*. (Berkeley, CA: Ten Speed Press, 2013).

Katz, Sandor Ellix. *Wild Fermentation: The Flavor, Nutrition, and Craft of Live-Culture Foods*. (White River Junction, VT: Chelsea Green Publishing, 2003).

Katz, Sandor Ellix. *The Art of Fermentation: An In-Depth Exploration of Essential Concepts and Processes from Around the World*. (White River Junction, VT: Chelsea Green Publishing, 2012).

Kulp, Karel, and Klaus Lorenz, eds. *Handbook of Dough Fermentations*. (New York, NY: Marcel Dekker, 2003).

Lewin, Alex. *Real Food Fermentation: Preserving Whole Fresh Food with Live Cultures in Your Home Kitchen*. (Beverly, MA: Quarry Books, 2012).

Pollan, Michael. *Cooked: A Natural History of Transformation*. (New York, NY: Penguin Press HC, 2013).

Robertson, Chad. *Tartine Bread*. (San Francisco, CA: Chronicle Books, 2010).

Robertson, Chad. *Tartine Book No. 3: Modern Ancient Classic Whole*. (San Francisco, CA: Chronicle Books, 2013).

Shurtleff, William. *The Book of Tempeh*. (Berkeley, CA: Ten Speed, 1979).

Shurtleff, William. *The Book of Miso*. (Berkeley, CA: Ten Speed, 2001).

Steinkraus, Keith, ed. *Handbook of Indigenous Fermented Foods*. (Boca Raton, FL: CRC Press, 1995).

Steinkraus, Keith, ed. *Industrialization of Indigenous Fermented Foods*. (New York, NY: Marcel Dekker, 2009).

Tamang, Jyoti Prakash, and Kasipathy Kailasapathy, eds. *Fermented Foods and Beverages of the World*. (Boca Raton, FL: CRC Press, 2010).

Tamang, Jyoti Prakash. *Himalayan Fermented Foods: Microbiology, Nutrition, and Ethnic Values*. (Boca Raton, FL: CRC Press, 2010).

Tamime, Adnan, ed. *Fermented Milks*. (Ames, IA: Blackwell Science Ltd, 2006).

Uvezian, Sonia. *The Book of Yogurt*. (New York, NY: Ecco, 1999).

Standard U.S./Metric Conversion Chart

VOLUME CONVERSIONS

U.S. Volume Measure	Metric Equivalent
⅛ teaspoon	0.5 milliliter
¼ teaspoon	1 milliliter
½ teaspoon	2 milliliters
1 teaspoon	5 milliliters
½ tablespoon	7 milliliters
1 tablespoon (3 teaspoons)	15 milliliters
2 tablespoons (1 fluid ounce)	30 milliliters
¼ cup (4 tablespoons)	60 milliliters
⅓ cup	90 milliliters
½ cup (4 fluid ounces)	125 milliliters
⅔ cup	160 milliliters
¾ cup (6 fluid ounces)	180 milliliters
1 cup (16 tablespoons)	250 milliliters
1 pint (2 cups)	500 milliliters
1 quart (4 cups)	1 liter (about)

WEIGHT CONVERSIONS

U.S. Weight Measure	Metric Equivalent
½ ounce	15 grams
1 ounce	30 grams
2 ounces	60 grams
3 ounces	85 grams
¼ pound (4 ounces)	115 grams
½ pound (8 ounces)	225 grams
¾ pound (12 ounces)	340 grams
1 pound (16 ounces)	454 grams

OVEN TEMPERATURE CONVERSIONS

Degrees Fahrenheit	Degrees Celsius
200 degrees F	95 degrees C
250 degrees F	120 degrees C
275 degrees F	135 degrees C
300 degrees F	150 degrees C
325 degrees F	160 degrees C
350 degrees F	180 degrees C
375 degrees F	190 degrees C
400 degrees F	205 degrees C
425 degrees F	220 degrees C
450 degrees F	230 degrees C

BAKING PAN SIZES

U.S.	Metric
8 × 1½ inch round baking pan	20 × 4 cm cake tin
9 × 1½ inch round baking pan	23 × 3.5 cm cake tin
11 × 7 × 1½ inch baking pan	28 × 18 × 4 cm baking tin
13 × 9 × 2 inch baking pan	30 × 20 × 5 cm baking tin
2 quart rectangular baking dish	30 × 20 × 3 cm baking tin
15 × 10 × 2 inch baking pan	30 × 25 × 2 cm baking tin (Swiss roll tin)
9 inch pie plate	22 × 4 or 23 × 4 cm pie plate
7 or 8 inch springform pan	18 or 20 cm springform or loose bottom cake tin
9 × 5 × 3 inch loaf pan	23 × 13 × 7 cm or 2 lb narrow loaf or pâté tin
1½ quart casserole	1.5 liter casserole
2 quart casserole	2 liter casserole

ABOUT THE AUTHOR

Branden Byers is the founder of FermUp.com, a blog and weekly podcast about anything and everything fermented. He spends a lot of time thinking, talking, and writing about fermented foods when not photographing or eating them. With an educational background in playwriting, masks, and puppet making, it is safe to assume that Branden spent many years working in restaurants. Over time this nurtured a strong appreciation for high-quality and thought-provoking foods. Having fermented foods at home for years, Branden realized it was time to share this knowledge and enthusiasm for the history, science, and culinary aspects of fermentation with others. He continues to spread fermented ideas around the globe from his home base in Madison, Wisconsin.

INDEX